THE TEN COMMANDMENTS
formerly

GOD'S FRONTIERS

By the same author:

WHAT MAKES A LEADER

IT'S A GREAT LIFE

FINDING THE WAY

CHRISTIAN ANSWERS ABOUT DOCTRINE

WHO DIED WHY

THE TROUBLED MIND

TO TELL YOU THE TRUTH

UNDERSTANDING
THE TEN COMMANDMENTS

formerly

GOD'S FRONTIERS

by John Eddison

SCRIPTURE UNION
47 Marylebone Lane, London, W1M 6AX

© John Eddison 1972

First published 1972
Reprinted 1977

All rights reserved. No part of this publication may be reproduced, stored in a retrieval system, or transmitted, in any form or by any means, electronic, mechanical, photocopying, recording or otherwise, without the prior permission of Scripture Union.

ISBN 0 85421 3821

CONTENTS

1.	No Absolute Standard?	7
2.	What the Situation Demands?	14
3.	No Rivals	24
4.	The Wrong Image	32
5.	The Traitor	41
6.	A Day to Remember	48
7.	Parents and Similar Problems	58
8.	If Looks Could Kill...	67
9.	Happily Ever After	78
10.	A Theft by any Other Name	88
11.	The Truth, the Whole Truth...	95
12.	If Only I Had...	102
13.	The Environmental Problem	109
14.	The Golden Rule	119

1. NO ABSOLUTE STANDARD?

You sometimes hear people say that it doesn't matter what we believe, so long as we behave in a reasonable way. 'Let's scrap all these dogmas,' they tell us, 'and just teach people to live good lives, and then all will be well.'

It sounds fine until we look at it a little more closely and discover that in fact a man's behaviour depends upon what he happens to believe. How I live physically, for example, will be influenced by what I believe about such things as hygiene, diet and medicine; and in the same way my moral life will depend upon whether or not I believe in the existence of a God to whom I must one day give an account of myself.

If I am an atheist, then obviously I won't expect there to be any absolute moral standards; for human behaviour will simply be the outcome of such things as heredity and environment, custom and tradition. But if on the other hand I am a Christian, then I shall view things differently. I shall expect God to have drawn up some sort of highway code, and it will come as no great surprise when I am told that this is outlined in the Ten Commandments, and then expanded and interpreted in other parts of the Bible.

I shall find, too, that this Law of God, as it is

usually called, is perfectly reasonable. It is not the whim of a capricious tyrant, but a set of rules lovingly laid down by the Maker Himself, who knew what was best for His creatures, and knew that they could only be happy and united if they observed it.

In fact we may say that it is not only divine, but natural—not only decreed by God Himself, but discerned in the natural order of things; for it stands to reason that if men went around murdering or stealing or running off with each other's wives, there would be a complete breakdown of social life and order, and no hope of progress. In other words, it isn't only that you can't do these things without risking God's punishment, but you cannot even do them without punishing yourself, any more than you can put your hand in the fire without being burned.

Putting the two together, therefore, we find that the Law of God agrees with the Law of Nature. We are told to do only what it is obvious that in our own interests we should do. A law which flies in the face of nature is a bad law, and bound to collapse. Cricket would be an impossible game to play, for example, if its laws were framed in such a way that they took no account of the law of gravity, but assumed that the ball, once hit into the air, would never come down again.

We can look at it another way. If a country is going to live at peace with its neighbours, one of the first things that must be settled is the question of its frontiers. Unless it knows exactly where these run, it will find itself trespassing on the territory of the country next door, and this in turn could lead to disputes and war. Now this is what the Law of God does for us. It marks the frontiers between ourselves and our fellow-men, and if we all observed these frontiers, then there would be permanent peace and good will; for 'good fences make good friends'.

But as we have already observed, these frontiers are not only legal, but natural as well. Some countries are divided from each other by artificial and unsatisfactory frontiers—just a line on a map which takes no account of geographical features. Between other countries there runs a river, or a range of mountains, or even a sea which forms a sensible, natural and easily recognized barrier. The frontiers mapped out for us by the Law of God are of the second kind. They are natural as well as moral. They are aimed at our common sense as well as at our conscience.

A hundred years ago these frontiers were generally accepted. That is not to say there was no trespassing. There was probably as much stealing and adultery per head of the population as there is today, but the point is that people knew they were trespassing. They recognized the frontiers, even if they did not like them and refused to observe them, and sometimes their consciences found it quite a painful business to climb over a kind of moral barbed-wire fence.

Things are very different today. People are telling us that the frontiers are out-of-date, that they no longer apply, and that we don't need them any more. 'We've grown up,' they say, 'and ought to be able to manage without rules. It doesn't really matter what we do, so long as we don't harm anyone else.' What accounts for this change of attitude? The answer is that most people have dispensed with the Christian faith which was the foundation of the older values. Changed beliefs have led to changed behaviour, and this ought not to surprise us greatly, for we have already seen how closely creed and conduct are linked together.

We have an extreme example of how this process works in pre-war Germany. For a long time we thought we could talk with the Nazis on the basis of moral equality; that is to say, that they believed those things to be right which we, as a nominally Christian country, believed to be right. We blamed them for disobeying a standard which they had long since abandoned; and they had abandoned it because as a nation they had rejected the Christian faith on which it was founded. From her own point of view Germany's behaviour was quite logical. We expected her to 'play the game', and she was doing so, only it happened to be a completely different game from the one we were trying to play; and, of course, the same rules could not be applied to it.

I saw a poster outside a church recently which said, 'You can't make good without God.' In other words, if you leave God out of account, then sooner or later you are going to produce a new pattern of behaviour, a new moral coinage. What is good or evil will no longer be decided by reference to God, but by the requirements of the state, the business or the individual. Principle will give way to expediency, and the end will begin to justify the means. This is because there is a fundamental flaw in human nature which makes it natural for us to gravitate towards what is evil. Although we have advanced in so many ways, we have never outgrown this tendency. As someone has said, 'Barbarism is not behind us, it is beneath us.'

The tragedy is that man cannot see where his own

best interests lie, for so much of the social unrest and disorder from which we suffer is the result of this overthrow of absolute moral standards. It is fashionable to deride the way in which the Old Testament equates godliness and prosperity—the reward of the righteous being material wealth, while poverty and suffering await the wicked. It is fair to say that this is only one aspect of the teaching of the Old Testament, (which roundly condemns materialism as such), but it is an important one; for godliness does breed those qualities of thrift, industry, and integrity which tend to exalt a country and lead to national prosperity.

We are often told, for example, that if only we had more money, we could put right many of the evils which afflict us, and this is no doubt true; for better houses, more hospitals and schools, and larger pensions all depend upon the amount of money available. There is equally no doubt that if we were an honest nation, many of these claims could be met. But what is the actual state of affairs? Every year something like £100m worth of goods are stolen from the shops in Britain. We are fast becoming a nation of shop-lifters rather than shop-keepers. And if to this considerable sum we add what is lost each year through evasion of TV licences, tax-fiddling, customs-dodging and so on, we quickly arrive at a figure which would make quite a difference to our standard of living.

If these benefits flowed from eradicating dishonesty in all its forms, what else might not follow if we could get rid of greed, laziness, selfishness and intemperance? Not only would we be better off ourselves, but we in Britain would be able to afford a much bigger proportion of our gross national product than the miserable 1 per cent we contribute at present to help under-privileged countries.

But why can't these things be put right by legislation? Up to a point, some of them can. But the law can often be too easily evaded. And the law is sometimes so costly to apply. And you cannot legislate against things like greed and selfishness and the basic weaknesses of human nature. That is why the Christian insists that what is wanted is a change of heart—not only legislation but regeneration.

Take an illustration from motoring. What is called 'Motorway Madness' can to some extent be checked by legislation, but no amount of new rules can change a bad driver and make him into a good one who will proceed with 'due care and attention'. What can the law say to the man who says, 'This is my car and I shall drive it how I like'? It can only reply, 'Then your blood be on your own head.'

It is just here that the Christian has something vitally important to say. 'It isn't your car,' he says, 'it was lent to you.' The Christian believes that he belongs to God and is accountable to Him. God will want to know how we have treated and used His car, and not just what damage we have managed to avoid doing with it.

It is when a man responds to this fact—that he has been made for God and that he belongs to Him—that this change of heart is brought about. And when this takes place, he begins to find that he looks at the Law of God in a new way. He tries to keep it not simply because it is advisable to do so, or even reasonable, but because it is desirable. '*I must*' has matured into '*I ought*', and that in turn to '*I want*'.

This is what Paul meant when he said, 'Love is the fulfilling of the law' (Romans 13. 10). If we love God, then we shall do what He wants and automatically fulfil His law, just as the man who drives carefully will observe the Highway Code without even thinking about it.

2. WHAT THE SITUATION DEMANDS?

THE Christian sees no conflict between God's law and His love. It is because the manufacturer has a sense of pride and respect for the car he has made that he issues a book of rules for its use; and we, too, live in a structured or ordered universe in which God's rules are a mark of His love, because they show His desire for our welfare and happiness.

It is love, too, which leads the Christian to try to obey God's laws. He doesn't simply do so out of a sense of duty, like a servant or a soldier, but with the loving response of a son; for, as we saw in the last chapter, 'love is the fulfilling of the law' (Romans 13. 10)—the reason, that is to say, for keeping it.

But what are we to say about those situations in which it would appear that the most loving course of action towards someone lies in the breaking of God's law? What about those cases when divorce seems the only possible answer to a marriage which has gone hopelessly wrong? What should we do when we are advised that it is best to mislead a patient about the true state of his health? Is a lie justified if it would save the life of a friend, or killing in time of war, or theft if it is the only way of bringing food to a starving person?

Does this mean that right and wrong are not

determined by any objective standard, but depend entirely upon the circumstances which prevail at the time? There are some who think so, and it has led them to accept a system of behaviour which is known as 'Situation Ethics'. It may be summed up as follows: there is only one course of action which is always right, regardless of the context, and that is the one which is dictated by love. This means that in any given situation you decide what is the right thing to do not by asking the question, 'What has God said?' but the question 'What does love suggest?'

Christians have always recognized the fact that there are circumstances in which it is necessary to choose the lesser of two evils, and when this is the case, they will almost certainly be guided by whichever course appears to be the more loving. But this pragmatic approach does not satisfy the situationalist. He will have nothing to do with the law. He admits that it may provide useful guidelines for human behaviour, but nothing more. Everything is justified by love, because where love is the motive, what might otherwise have been sin ceases to be so.

If we go back to the analogy of motoring, we all know that there may be certain circumstances in which we feel justified in breaking the speed limit—if, for example, we are trying to get someone to hospital or to prevent a crime. But this does not invalidate the laws of motoring, and we don't feel hardly done by if we are caught and have to pay a fine, because we realize that it would be much worse to have no rules at all than to have rules which can in exceptional cases be broken.

Bishop Robinson has called 'Situation Ethics' 'the

only ethic for man come of age'. But has man come of age? Scientifically and intellectually he may have done, but in moral and spiritual ways he is still very immature, and still needs to be governed by rules. If we could eradicate every grain of recklessness and stupidity from every motorist in the country, then perhaps we could do away with the Highway Code and substitute the one word—'Care'. And if we could remove from the heart of man every trace of pride, greed, lust, cruelty and selfishness, then perhaps we could talk of his 'coming of age', and then we might be able to use the word 'Love', not just as a summary of the Ten Commandments (which is how Jesus used it), but as a substitute. But is anyone seriously going to suggest that we are yet within a million years of such maturity?

But let us come back to our previous question. What are we to do in those situations in which law and love seem to be opposed, or one of the rules conflicts with another? It might be helpful at this stage to cite four examples of the problem we are facing; these examples involve the sixth, seventh, eighth and ninth commandments respectively.

Claus von Stauffenberg was a devout Roman Catholic who plotted the assassination of Hitler because he was convinced that the man was utterly evil and for the sake of Germany must be exterminated. The plot failed on July 20th, 1944, and the conspirators, including Dietrich Bonhoeffer, were executed. But the question remains: were they right to try? Did the circumstances justify assassination or murder?

The second example concerns a woman who was taken prisoner by the Russians at the end of the last war, and prevented from joining her husband and family in Germany. She was told that she could be released and restored to them if she became chronically sick or pregnant, and so, with the obliging help of a friendly guard, she took the latter course. In due time she was allowed to return to Germany where she and her baby were rapturously welcomed by her family, who completely approved of what she had done. But we are bound to ask: was she right or wrong? Did the circumstances justify adultery?

My third example is imaginary. Let us suppose that you know someone who is intent upon causing a serious injury to another person against whom he has a grudge. You slip into the cloakroom where his coat is hanging, or you break into his house when he is away from home, and you remove the weapon with which he intended to make the attack. Did you do right or wrong? Did the circumstances justify theft?

My last illustration concerns the ninth commandment—'Thou shalt not bear false witness...' Should Jeanie Deans, in Sir Walter Scott's novel *The Heart of Midlothian,* have lied at her sister's trial if it was the only way of establishing her innocence? And should Rahab have told the King of Jericho a string of lies to prevent his capturing the spies whom (for very good reasons) she had welcomed and concealed (Joshua 2)? Did the circumstances justify bearing false witness?

It is difficult to believe that there are Christians who would put a straight ruler against these very crooked situations and come up immediately with a rigid, legalistic verdict; but at the same time it would be dangerous to assume without very careful thought that the commandment must in each case be overruled in the interests of humanity.

The first thing that needs to be said is that the examples we have chosen are very extreme—contrived, we might almost say, for the purposes of argument. They describe situations in which we are very unlikely to find ourselves, and even if we were satisfied that in each case the commandment should be broken, we would not have proved that the Law of God was invalid. Hard cases make bad law, and very often it is the exception that proves the rule.

Secondly, we note that in some cases the conflict is not between two commandments, but between legality and humanity. In the Christian view international peace (which might have followed Hitler's assassination) and family unity, although highly desirable, are not actual commandments, and there could arise circumstances when too high a price is demanded for them.

In the next place, the Christian would want to satisfy himself that there was no possible third course open to him. In the case of the homicidal neighbour, for example, could the police have been informed and legal entry made into the man's house? Could Hitler have been kidnapped? Perhaps there is no third way, but at least the possibility should be explored before we assume too readily that it is right to break God's law.

It is surprising, for example, how often a little forethought will help us to avoid the telling of a direct lie. Of course, we have to be careful to avoid the attempt to deceive—what Kipling calls 'the truthful, well-weighed answer that tells the blacker lie.' But we usually lie because we are caught off our guard and, given time to think, there is often a middle course which we can adopt between deceiving one person and, let us say, betraying another.

Then again we need to consider very carefully the effect of involving others in what we do. Take the case of the German woman who wanted to get back to her family. Granted for the purpose of this argument that she was justified on her own account in doing what she did, we are still left wondering whether or not she ought to have involved the guard, however willing he was. By causing someone else to offend, we may be storing up trouble for him in the future; for long afterwards he may come to regard what he has done in a less favourable light, and remember it with bitter regret. It is always risky to expose another person to the possible backlash of an action whose consequences we cannot foresee at the time.

There is an important extension to this argument. A Christian must ask himself what are likely to be the repercussions of his actions, how far the ripples are going to travel, and what inferences can be drawn from it. He is like the motorist who must decide whether by rushing his friend to the hospital he is endangering other people on the road. It is interesting to note, for example, that Sir Winston Churchill declared himself against assassination, even in war time, because he felt that it could provide a precedent for the overthrow of law and order in other countries. Indeed, if we could ever find Bishop Robinson's ideal Christian—'Man come of age'—we would I think be struck by the care he took lest his own liberty should lead others astray (I Corinthians 8. 9). There might be some things which he personally would feel justified in doing, but would refrain from for the sake of others.

It is safe to say, therefore, at this stage of the argument that if murder, adultery, theft or false witness are ever justified, it can only be in very exceptional cases; after every other conceivable escape route from a seemingly impossible situation has been explored; when we have fully weighed up the short- and long-term consequences, and have satisfied ourselves that these are beneficial or at least neutral in effect; and when the motive is one of love.

We must now begin to examine more closely just what we mean by love, because it is in the name of love that such actions as we have been considering are justified, if they are justified at all. The New Testament has four words to describe love. There is sexual love (eros), family love (storge), brotherly love (philia) and Christian love (agape).

It is the last of these that concerns us here, and this kind of love refers to the will rather than to the emotions. Bishop Stephen Neill has described it as 'the steady directing of the human will towards the eternal well-being of another' or, we may add, to the glory of God. And Dr. Dodd has said that 'it is not primarily an emotion or affection; it is primarily an active determination of the will. That is why it can be commanded, as feelings cannot.' In other words, if I love someone in a Christian way, it means that I will want the very best for that person, even though it could involve him in suffering and disappointment.

This sort of love can land us in some rather disturbing situations, as for example when I have to tell a friend who is hopelessly in love that he is heading towards a disastrous marriage; or when a doctor thinks that a patient ought to be told how desperately ill he is, because only in that way will he face the reality of death and prepare himself for it. Love of this kind is the very opposite of the sentimental desire to see someone enjoying a short-term happiness at the expense of his own ultimate good.

We can be quite sure that it was a genuine love for his country which led von Stauffenberg to try to kill Hitler. But did he choose the best possible way of expressing that love? Might it have been in the best interests of Germany that she should drink the cup of suffering to the dregs and see in her defeat the unmistakable judgement of God? Bonhoeffer thought so at one time, for in 1939 he told a friend that, 'If you want to know the truth, I pray for the defeat of my nation, for I believe that it is the only way to pay for the suffering it has caused the world.'

It is interesting that Professor Joseph Fletcher and other writers on this subject have little to say about love towards God. They have a lot to say about the 'horizontal' dimension of love, but nothing very much about its 'vertical' one. But if I love God as I ought to do, may I not sometimes have to choose holiness of life rather than happiness—even the happiness of those I love?

We can have every sympathy for the woman held prisoner in Russia; and few would like to condemn her for the action she took. At the same time, would we feel any less respect for her if she had felt that the sacrifice of her virtue was too big a price to pay for her release? Or if she had reason to believe that her husband would not welcome her home on such terms? Would she have deserved Mark Twain's description—'A good woman in the worst sense of the word'? Surely if her decision was the result of her love for God and her desire to please Him, even if it meant hurting others, it could deserve nothing but praise.

There are I think three things which need to be said in conclusion. First, as we have seen, the word 'love' has so many shades of meaning and is so personal and subjective, that in practice it is very often almost impossible to know what it suggests as being the right course of action. What God's law does for us is to define what love involves, so that we are provided with a clear, objective guide to conduct rather than one which is woolly and highly subjective.

Secondly, it is very easy to discuss all this without reference to the grace of God. History is full of examples of the way in which He has met people in the most desperate situations and answered their prayers; and there are innumerable instances of how those who have refused to by-pass His road to happiness have been rewarded.

It is interesting to notice how this whole area of divine activity is left unexplored by the advocates of 'Situation Ethics'. Solutions are always sought on a human level, and not nearly enough allowance is made for the activity of God in the world He has created. But God is at work in history. He does engineer circumstances. 'Coincidences' do happen in answer to prayer, and 'all things work together for good' to those who love Him (Romans 8. 28).

It was in this spirit of faith and prayer that some of the great men and women of the Bible like Joseph, David, Daniel and others were able to find the right path to take; and I would like to feel that, faced with the sort of dilemmas we have been considering, I could trust God to reveal His way out of the impasse. But if He does not do so, and we are finally faced with the choice between two evils, then we must ask Him to show us which is the lesser of the two, and which course of action is indicated by love for Him and love for our fellow-men and women.

Finally, if we do have to make such a choice, and deem it to be the right one in the circumstances, we must not pretend to ourselves that it is intrinsically good. We will still have sinned, even though we honestly believe that the sin is less grievous than it would have been if we had taken the other course; and because we have sinned, we shall need to ask for forgiveness. It may have been necessary to break the speed limit, but the fine must still be paid. It is interesting to note in this connexion that, on the night before he set off to Hitler's Headquarters with the fateful bomb, von Stauffenberg visited a church for a time of prayer; and, knowing the man, there can be little doubt that he prayed for forgiveness for the crime which he sincerely felt it was his duty to commit.

3. NO RIVALS

We must now turn to the Ten Commandments themselves. We must try to remember that they are not just a number of isolated rules, but the foundation on which the whole of Christian behaviour has been constructed; and it is only in the context of the Bible as a whole that they can be properly understood.

If you have looked at primitive paintings, you will know how flat and 'two-dimensional' they appear. There is height and breadth all right, but it was only very much later on, when the rules of perspective were understood, that any idea of depth began to appear.

In rather the same way it is only in the New Testament, with the life and teaching of Jesus, that the full spiritual content of the law is seen—touching thought and feeling, as well as word and deed. The Commandments provided an outline map of God's Kingdom, but it was left to Jesus Himself to fill in the details; and this is what He meant when He said 'Think not that I am come to destroy the Law, or the prophets: I am not come to destroy, but to fulfil'. (Matthew 5. 17).

It will therefore be our task to try to discover the full spiritual implications of the Ten Commandments. Standing by themselves they look fairly simple and uncomplicated, like the tips of so many icebergs; but in the light of what we find in other parts of the Bible, we shall see how deeply they really go, and how they affect almost every aspect and department of human behaviour.

The Ten Commandments divide themselves into two groups. The first group, comprising Commandments 1-4, deals with our relationship to God; and the second group (Commandments 5-10) deals with our relationship to one another—and affects what we do (5-8), what we say (9), and what we are (10). You will find them fully set out in Exodus 20. 1-17.

So we come to the first of the Ten Commandments—'Thou shalt have no other gods before Me.' In other words, God is commanding us to make Him supreme, the one and only object of our worship, our faith and our love, and that we are to have no other gods in addition to Himself. The 'country' of our lives is not to be an 'oligarchy', ruled over by several different and perhaps competing masters; but a 'monarchy', in which He Himself is allowed to reign alone and supreme. It is asking quite a lot, isn't it? And before we decide what to do, we shall want to know a little more about the God who makes this demand for the exclusive ownership of our lives.

I—I AM

It is interesting to notice that when God gave this first commandment, He began by introducing Himself as follows—'I am the Lord thy God . . .' He reminds us of His existence. But can we be sure that there is a God? It is one of the basic instincts of human nature that we must find something to worship and serve, and even the atheist Voltaire admitted that 'If there were no God, it would be necessary to invent one.' But can this instinct be satisfied, like the others we possess, or is it there just to mock us and tantalize us?

In another book (*To Tell You the Truth*), I have tried to answer this question more fully, and to show that the evidence in favour of God's existence can carry us beyond all reasonable doubt. If there is no God, how do we account for the origin of the universe and the order which we observe all around us? If there is no God, what is the explanation of man? From where did he get his reason, his conscience and his soul? If there is no God, what are we to make of the Bible? And how can we explain the life of Jesus Christ, His miraculous birth, His sinlessness and His resurrection? Of course, these things do not add up to a positive, mathematical proof that there is a God. We cannot expect that kind of answer. But they do make it perfectly reasonable for intelligent people to believe that there is a supreme personal being who made the universe and everything in it, and who is therefore a proper object of our faith and love.

II—I ACT

Notice how God's introduction continues: 'I am the Lord thy God, which brought thee out of the land of Egypt, out of the house of bondage . . .' In other words, the Jews believed in a God who not only existed, but who had also acted; for they had experienced something of His love and power when He delivered them from Egypt.

Perhaps like the Jews of old we can think of times in our lives when we have been conscious of God's hand guiding and guarding us. 'Thank God,' we have said, when some calamity has been avoided, or some unexpected success has come our way. It was not just an empty form of words. We have honestly felt, just for a moment, that God was with us, shaping our lives. We have realized that we are indebted to Him for our 'creation, preservation and all the blessings of this life'.

But we are in a much stronger position than those who lived long ago. We are not like the Athenians whom Paul reproved because they built an altar to 'The unknown God' (Acts 17. 23). The God whom we worship has intervened in history, and made Himself known to us in the person of our Lord Jesus Christ. We can look back upon a far greater deliverance than that of the Jews from Egypt. God has entered this world in human form, and allowed Himself to suffer death for our redemption. Therefore it is not some remote, uninterested deity who commands our obedience, but a God who has shown His infinite love towards us by coming to our rescue, and by suffering upon the cross to bring us forgiveness and freedom; and to those who keep asking 'Why doesn't God do something?' we can point to Jesus Christ as the unmistakable proof of God's activity in the world.

III—I ASK

The reasoning behind the first commandment is as follows: 'Because I am ... and because I have ... therefore thou shalt ...' It has a twofold authority, the authority of His person and of His work. On the strength of who He is and on the strength of what He has done He says, 'Thou shalt have no other gods in addition to Me.'

And yet, the fact remains that this commandment

is widely disregarded. Why is this? Is it unbelief? Surely not! It is true that there are honest agnostics who say that they cannot believe in the existence of God, but as Bacon said, 'Atheism is rather in the life than in the heart of man.' He meant that men and women break the first commandment, not because they do not believe in God, but because they do not want Him. The trouble is not so much unbelief as unwillingness. They prefer the 'other gods'.

What are the 'other gods'? At the time when the Ten Commandments were first given, of course, the ideas of men were very primitive. Each tribe and country would have a different god. Names like Ammon, Ashtoreth, Baal, Chemosh and Moloch frequently appear in the Old Testament. Sometimes they were worshipped singly, and sometimes in groups. Later on we find that the ancient Greeks and Romans had their gods, each one often responsible for a different department of life, rather like ministers of state. Thus Mars was the god of war, Venus of love, Bacchus of pleasure, and so on. Men worshipped these gods, often with debased and corrupt rites, and sought their help.

It is easy to blame such people, and to imagine that we have advanced a long way beyond their depraved ideas, but have we really done so? True, the names of their ancient gods have ceased to exist, but very often the things they stood for are still popular, and can twine their way round the hearts of people, and threaten the supremacy of the true God. What ancient Greek or Roman, for example, visiting some drunken orgy would believe that Bacchus was dead? Or reading in the newspapers about sexual licence would not suppose Venus to be as alive and active as ever?

And to these ancient gods of pleasure and sex, modern man has added others of his own. There are people whose chief object in life is to make as much money as possible. There are others who have no time for God because they are so absorbed in their business, their families or their gardens. While others of us, to whom these things make as yet little appeal, have begun manufacturing 'gods' out of hobbies, motor-bikes, girl-friends, games or music. All these things, many of them excellent in themselves, can become the modern equivalents of the primitive gods of days gone by. They rival the God who made heaven and earth. They challenge His authority. They steal the loyalty and affection which should belong to Him alone.

Have you any 'other gods or goddesses'? You can find the answer to that question by asking yourself another one: 'What is the last possession from which I would want to be parted?' Work slowly through a list of your treasures, in an ascending order of preciousness, and see what you are left with at the end: my allowance, my record-player, my motor-bike, my boy-friend or girl-friend, my place in the team, my popularity, my job, my . . . . Is there anything left? Have you still got your faith in God? If you have, then you are obeying this first commandment; but if you have not, and other things are more precious than He is, then you are not doing so; one of the 'other gods' has taken his place at the top of the list.

What must we do if we are not obeying this commandment, but really want to do so? We must do two things. We must turn and we must take. We must abandon and we must accept. There must be a negative step and a positive one. We must get rid of the other gods, just as Moses ordered the golden calf to be smashed in the wilderness (Exodus 32. 20); and we must yield ourselves wholeheartedly to God. He will not share His throne with any rivals. He asks for sovereign control, and complete paramountcy.

This is a very serious decision. In fact it is a matter of life and death. Some people speak as though God had given us 'Ten Suggestions' instead of 'Ten Commandments'. They look upon Him as a kind of optional extra, like the heater in a car—nice to have if you can afford it, and a comfort to the elderly and infirm, but not absolutely necessary. In answer to this popular, casual, easy-going attitude there are two things to say. First, without God there is no real meaning or purpose in life. It is not just that the car is less comfortable without Him but it will not even start. There is no contact and therefore no life in the engine. The steering is totally unreliable and there is no power in the brakes.

There are many objects in life which only make sense and fulfil the purpose of their existence if they are related to something else. Thus an electric stove must be plugged into the socket, a bullet fitted into the rifle, and an L.P. placed on the record-player. Unless these connections are made, all you have is a useless ornament.

Man, too, belongs to this class of object. 'Oh, God,' said St. Augustine, 'Thou hast made us for Thyself and our hearts are restless until they find repose in Thee.' Man's *'raison d'être'* is to be identified with

God and personally connected with Him by faith (Isaiah 43. 21). We have been made for a purpose—to know God and to enjoy Him for ever; and therefore without Him life becomes meaningless and hollow.

To deprive ourselves of this one source of true happiness and peace is bad enough, but even more serious is the fact that continued disobedience to this commandment must bring the judgment of God upon us. We can break some rules, and, if we are lucky, get away with it; but we cannot do that with the laws of God. If we persist in ignoring Him and disobeying His commands, then we cannot escape the inevitable consequences. We are told that 'the wages of sin is death' (Romans 6. 23). That is to say, the penalty for choosing to live without God in this life is that we shall be compelled to live without Him in the next.

4. THE WRONG IMAGE

A CLERGYMAN walked into his church one day, and saw an old tramp studying the Ten Commandments which were painted on one of the walls. He was about to speak to him, when the old man turned round, and began to shuffle out of the church, muttering to himself, 'Well, anyway, I've never made a graven image.' He was prepared to plead guilty to the other nine commandments, but he felt fairly safe so far as Number 2 was concerned.

Perhaps he was right. Probably very few of us have made a 'graven image' of anything, and even if we have, we have not felt that we have done anything very terrible. After all, if this commandment is to be taken literally, think of all the statues, busts and even paintings which would have to be destroyed in our cities, cathedrals and museums.

But of course that is not the point. Moses allowed the carving of heavenly beings and flowers, and on one occasion was commanded to make a serpent of brass, and set it up in the middle of the camp (Numbers 21); and Solomon adorned the temple with carvings of flowers and trees. The whole point of the second commandment was to forbid the worship of God under a material form, and to protect His essentially spiritual character, His holiness and majesty. It was only many years later, in the days of

Hebrew degeneracy, that a narrow literalism pressed this commandment into a complete ban on painting and sculpture, with the result that the Jews have contributed so little in that field compared with what they have given the world in music and literature.

The first commandment requires us to believe in and worship God, and the second commandment requires us to think of Him in the right way. It has a double application. The ancient error was to try to represent God in a material way; the modern error is to have a false or inadequate mental image of what He is really like. We will consider them each in turn.

I—THE MATERIAL IMAGE

The minds of primitive people were full of the idea of God. They felt His power in nature. The sun spoke of His favour, and the thunder of His wrath. But what was He like? How could they find words with which to convey the idea of Him to others? For such people words are clumsy tools, and so they used pictures instead. The lion suggested His strength, the eagle His wisdom, the crocodile, striking unseen in the water, His sudden anger.

It all began quite simply and innocently. What, after all, are idols but 'solid metaphors'? And men were only doing in wood and stone what we try to do with words. Why, therefore, were the Jews forbidden to make any graven image? For two very good reasons. First, it was *degrading to God*. It stands to reason that any human attempt to depict a God who is spiritual, immortal and invisible must be derogatory to His character. If even words fail us, how much more unsatisfactory are wood, ivory and stone?

Imagine trying to translate Shakespeare into some primitive language with a very limited vocabulary, or do justice to a Beethoven symphony on a mouth organ. It could not be done. The attempt would be an insult to Shakespeare and Beethoven. No one would have any idea what their true glory was really like. Far better to leave it to the imagination than degrade it by an unworthy reproduction.

In the second place this practice was *demoralizing to man*. All too soon what happened was this: the image began to take the place of God, and what may have started as an aid to worship became an object of worship. As Paul put it when writing to the Romans: 'They changed the glory of the uncorruptible God into an image made like to corruptible man, and to birds, and ... beasts ... and worshipped and served the creature more than the Creator' (Romans 1. 23, 25).

Once the image is substituted for what it represents, then God becomes something we can control, and there follows the temptation to use Him for our own ends. The little statue, the gold cross, the sacred relic become holy in themselves, capable of working miracles and protecting us from evil. In other words, God is reduced to the level of a mascot, carried about from place to place, and those who worship Him in this way become riddled with superstition.

It was from this kind of idolatry that God tried to preserve His people. Again and again they slipped back, infected by the heathen tribes all around them. Prophet after prophet appeared on the scene to call them back from their superstition and sin, and to re-kindle in their minds a truly spiritual and moral picture of God. 'To whom then will ye liken God?' they cried, 'or what likeness will ye compare unto Him?' (Isaiah 40. 18).

II--THE MENTAL IMAGE

We have largely grown out of that sort of thing today, though it is strange to find that superstition in some form or other often persists among quite educated people; and superstition is really a relic, a kind of vestigial remain of idolatry. But it is true to say that there are still false images of God in the world just as dangerous to true worship as the material images of old. I remember reading once of a small boy whose father had gone abroad to fight in a war, and whom he had never seen. All he had was a large photograph over the fireplace. To him this was 'Daddy'. When at long last his father returned, he had altered considerably, and was no longer like the photograph. The little boy refused to believe that he was his father. He kept pointing to the photograph and saying 'Daddy'. His mind had been conditioned by the photograph, and it was only after some time that the true and living image of his father prevailed.

So it is today that many people have false or inadequate images in their minds of what God is like. There is a book by J. B. Phillips called: *Your God is Too Small*. And that is perfectly true of the God whom many people worship. He is too small. In some vitally important respect He is lacking something.

There is first of all the *Sportsman* image. Here we have a friendly, indulgent figure who is far too kind and easy-going to want to interfere with human wrong-doing. In his view it is more important that we should have a good time than try to develop a good character, and his worshippers are confident that he will not judge too severely their desire to 'have a bit of fun', as they describe giving way to temptation. Then there is the *Policeman* image. This time we have the complete opposite—a God whose sole purpose is to uphold and enforce the law, and whose interest in us only begins when we break it. Again, there is the *Fireman* image, and people who create this particular idol think of God as someone on whom they can call in an emergency, when there is some great national or personal crisis, but who is neither required nor wanted in the normal way. Lastly, there is the *Spaceman* image. That is to say, a God who is remote, uninterested and out of touch. He may have had something to do with the world once, but now he is merely a distant and impersonal spectator, watching it roll on to its inevitable climax.

Now the trouble with all these images is not that they are one hundred per cent wrong (for they all contain a grain of truth), but that they are hopelessly inadequate. God certainly wants us to be happy; and of course He must uphold and apply the law. It goes without saying that He will come to our help in time of need: and it is perfectly true that in one sense He is utterly beyond us. But even if we could roll all these ideas into one, and multiply them a thousand times, we would still fall far short of our target. We would still be trying to translate Shakespeare into a primitive dialect, and play Beethoven on a mouth organ. People who think like this are really doing what the Jews were forbidden to do. They are making a false representation of God, and then worshipping the image they have set up.

It was more difficult for people in ancient days to get the right idea of God. They had to rely on what the prophets taught them, and it is not always easy to get a clear picture of someone whom you have never seen, when all you have to go upon are verbal descriptions. But all the same, by the time the Old Testament ends, they had a wonderfully clear outline of the character and nature of God.

We find, first of all, that *He is spiritual* (Psalm 139. 1-18). That means that He does not need to assume for His existence any material or corporal form. Next, we learn that *He is eternal* (Isaiah 57. 15). He is independent of time and space, and lives outside them, rather as an author lives outside the people and the events of his book. Then *He is moral* (Micah 6. 8). That means that He is intensely concerned with the way we behave, because He wants us to be like Himself, holy and good. Finally, we discover that *He is personal* (Psalm 103. 13, 14). He is interested in us, loves us, and cares for us like a father. Gradually these truths were revealed to the Jews, and as they dawned with increasing light upon their minds, so the desire for the old idols began to diminish. Faced with the true glory and beauty of the Lord, 'Ephraim shall say, What have I to do any more with idols? I have heard Him, and observed Him' (Hosea 14. 8).

But we today are immeasurably better off, even than the Jews who spoke like this, and have far less excuse for our unworthy mental images than ever they had for their unworthy material ones. Why is this? When Jesus Christ came into this world, He provided us with the one perfect and sufficient means of knowing what God is like; for to look at Christ and to think of Him is all that we need to do. He has given the authentic translation, the perfect reflection.

Perhaps an illustration will help. There are some substances which can exist in two forms—either in solution, or in the form of crystals. Common salt is a good example. You can have it in solution, in which case it is sea-water, or you can have it in crystal form in the salt cellar on the table. When it is in solution, it is invisible and intangible, and though you may have some idea of its presence, your knowledge of it is fairly limited. When you have it in crystals, on the other hand, you have it in a form which you can see and handle.

Now in the ordinary way God exists, so to speak, 'in solution'. He is invisible, inaudible, intangible. There is no one place in the universe to which we can point and say, 'He is there', nor can we speak of any place as 'God-forsaken', because 'He inhabiteth eternity' (Isaiah 57. 15).

What happened when Jesus Christ came into this world was that He presented God to man in what we might call 'crystalline form'. He made the eternal God visible, tangible and audible to ordinary human beings (1 John 1. 1. 2). He represented God to us in terms which we can understand; and looking at Christ we see, not the whole of God, because He is infinite and eternal, but as much of God as human beings are at present capable of knowing. As St. Paul says, 'In Him dwelleth all the fulness of the Godhead (in) bodily (form)' (Colossians 2. 9).

The TV presentation of some great event gives the home-bound viewer as much of it as he can possibly experience within the limits of his room, and Jesus presents His Father to us on a scale and in such a way that finite, earth-bound creatures can actually say they have seen God (John 14. 9). Or, thinking of an earlier illustration, it is as though Beethoven himself transcribed one of his symphonies so that it could be performed on a church organ.

Jesus Christ then is 'the image of the invisible God' (Colossians 1. 15), and if I want to know what God is like, I need to study the life of Jesus. I see Him healing the sick, raising the dead, casting out demons, feeding the multitude, walking on the water, and I realize that 'power belongeth unto God' (Psalm 62. 11). I listen to His teaching, and I discover 'the depth of the riches both of the wisdom and knowledge of God' (Romans 11. 33). I watch His life, and I find that He is never impatient, never selfish, never proud—in fact completely without sin; and I see that 'the Lord our God is holy' (Leviticus 19. 2). Finally, I follow Him to the upper room, to the garden, to the green hill and to the cross; I see Him suffer, and I hear His words of forgiveness and sympathy, and I know that 'God is love' (1 John 4. 8).

Instead of man's fumbling and imperfect ideas, we have in Jesus Christ the one and only official and faultless reproduction of God. He does not, of course, show us everything there is to know about God, but nothing that He does show us is in the slightest degree distorted or untrue. The writer to the Hebrews sums it up when he says that Jesus Christ is 'the brightness of God's glory, and the express (faultless) image of His person' (Hebrews 1. 3).

'Why is all this so important?' someone asks. 'I can see that it helps to have a proper image of God, but why is it made into a commandment?' We have really dealt with that question already, but let us look at it from a slightly different angle. In the first place, it is obviously dishonouring to God to worship Him or think of Him in any unworthy or inadequate way. If we found some primitive tribe in a remote corner of the Commonwealth whose people had a completely unlifelike portrait or photograph of the Queen, we would be quick to change it, because we would feel that in some way Her Majesty was being insulted. And that, only very much more so, is how we ought to feel about any idea of God which falls short of what is revealed to us in the Bible and in the life of Christ.

But there is a second reason, which concerns ourselves, and that is that we tend to grow like the God we worship. Writing about the heathen, the psalmist speaks of their idols, and then says, 'they that make them are like unto them; so is every one that trusteth in them' (Psalm 115. 2-8). If, for example, we entertain in our minds the 'Sportsman Image' of which we thought, then we shall tend to grow slack and casual about sin both in ourselves and others; while worshipping the 'Policeman Image' may make us censorious and critical and lacking in love and sympathy. If, on the other hand, we worship 'the God and Father of our Lord Jesus Christ' (Ephesians 1. 3), then we shall begin to grow like Him in holiness, wisdom, strength and love; and God's great purpose for all His creatures is that they should be 'conformed to the image of His Son' (Romans 8. 29).

5. THE TRAITOR

THE first commandment was aimed at the heart, the second at the mind, and the third at the tongue. What a traitor the tongue is! It betrays our nationality; for you only have to be in the presence of a foreigner for a few minutes before some quaintly pronounced word will tell you that he comes from abroad. In a quite different way it betrays our health, because the state of a person's tongue will often reveal his physical condition.

And what is true physically is true spiritually. A person who swears like the proverbial trooper is unlikely to be a member of God's Kingdom; for no one talks like that if he is really trying to honour and serve God. In the same way, we can tell that something is wrong with a person's moral health, with the spiritual condition of his heart, by his use of unclean or bad language; for 'out of the abundance of the heart the mouth speaketh' (Matthew 12. 34). No wonder James has so much to say about the tongue in his short letter! He tells us that it is like 'a fire' which may begin in a very small way but which can do untold damage; and like 'a fountain' from which flows a continual stream of words, sometimes good and sometimes bad (James 3). If only we could control the fire and keep the fountain fresh and clean, what perfect people we would be!

This commandment deals with one particular misuse of the tongue: 'Thou shalt not take the name of the Lord thy God in vain.' What exactly does that mean? Think first of all of the Name. It means far more than the three letters that compose it—G-O-D. It stands for character and reputation. First, it suggests *dignity*. A person's name distinguishes him from other people. It may be one which he or his ancestors have covered with glory by their achievements, and which he carries with pride. It is his property, and no one can take it from him. In the case of God His name is unique. There is no one else 'of that name'. It is 'the name which is above every name' (Philippians 2. 9), and belongs to the Creator, Preserver and Ruler of the universe.

Then His name stands for *authority*. 'Use my name', people sometimes say to us, and we know that the person's name carries authority and power. If you have a British passport, you will see that it bears the signature of the Foreign Secretary. It is in his name that you present yourself to customs officials, and are allowed to cross frontiers. God's name is like that. Everything in heaven and earth must one day give way to His authority, and acknowledge His power (Psalm 72. 17).

Thirdly, His name stands for *integrity*. We often speak of a firm or of an individual as 'having a good name'. We mean that they are people to be trusted, who will not fail us or let us down, and on whom we can rely completely. And God is like that. His name is beyond reproach. His word is utterly to be trusted. No wonder the psalmist said, 'O Lord, how excellent is Thy name in all the earth!' (Psalm 8. 9).

The word 'vain' means empty or hollow. A 'vain

threat' is one which we lack the power or the will to carry out. To 'look in vain' for something means that our search is unrewarded. To 'take the name of the Lord in vain' means to speak of Him, or of anything to do with Him, in a light-hearted, thoughtless, flippant way; for by doing so, we are in some measure dishonouring Him, and cheapening His dignity, authority and integrity. When we think of God or speak of Him we should always do so, as the hymn reminds us, 'with awe and wonder, and with bated breath'. There are three very common ways in which people break this commandment, and we will consider each in turn.

I—BLASPHEMY

This means the using of God's name as a swear-word. Most people who use expressions like 'O my God', or 'Christ', or 'Good Lord' would be horrified if you accused them of blasphemy. But that is really what it is. Gradually, perhaps, they have slipped into the habit, and now they find it almost too hard to break.

As we have seen, language of this sort, together with a whole range of other swear-words, betrays the true state of a person's mind. It suggests that the person concerned has never really crossed the frontier into God's kingdom, and that he is still a 'stranger' and a 'foreigner'. It suggests also that his heart needs to be cured from sin, because a good fountain would never produce poison of this kind.

Are you a victim of this habit? Then you must tackle the problem at its source. You must ask yourself whether you have ever really started the Christian life, and entered God's kingdom, and whether He has cleansed your heart from sin. Once He has become your King and Saviour, you will never want to use His name in that way again.

You will not want to, but at first it may be rather difficult to stop, if the thing has become a habit. Nature has done quite a lot to help us there. The tongue is not on the surface of our bodies, where everyone can see it, like the nose or the ears. It has been parked securely behind two thick lips and two strong rows of teeth. It is as though nature were saying to us, 'You are going to have some difficulty with this particular instrument, and so I am putting it under guard for you.'

The trouble is that most of us find these safeguards are not enough. We not only need a sentry, but a censor. It is just here that we shall find prayer such a help. The psalmist prayed, 'Set a watch, O Lord, before my mouth; keep the door of my lips' (Psalm 141. 3). That is a prayer we need to use constantly. The moment we feel the temptation to swear or to blaspheme, we must learn to send up a quick prayer for help: 'Lord, guard my lips.' If we can get into this habit, we shall find ourselves conquering the other one.

II—HYPOCRISY

Milton has called hypocrisy 'the only evil that walks invisible, except to God alone.' It means to act a part, pretending to be what we are not, and you will remember that it was the particular failing of the Pharisees in Jesus' day. They were very religious people, but all too often their religion was simply a veneer—a beautiful coating of mahogany over cheap and ordinary deal. Let us look at the two kinds of hypocrisy of which they were guilty.

Words without thoughts. Words are rather like coins. The £, for example, will buy far less today than it bought ten years ago. The reason is that its value has seriously deteriorated. It does not stand for what it used to stand for. So it is with words. They all too frequently devalue with use, and do not convey the meaning they should. How often we catch ourselves saying 'The Lord's Prayer' or 'Grace', and we realize that we have not been attending to our own words. 'What was that you said?' a friend of mine asked a boy in his class one day. 'I don't know, sir,' was the reply, 'I wasn't listening.' I am afraid that is how we often treat God. The words we use have too little behind them. They are hollow. They are vain, and like the Pharisees' prayers, they are a pretence (Mark 12. 40).

'I often say my prayers, but do I ever pray? And do the wishes of my heart go with the words I say?' So runs a children's hymn, but it asks two very practical and important questions and probably most of us have discovered that it needs real discipline and concentration to conquer this tendency. Some people have found that it helps to utter the words they use, if not aloud, at least forming them on the lips. Others find it helpful to write out their own prayers, or use prayers which others have written. There is certainly room for experiment in trying to overcome this danger of hypocrisy in prayer.

Words without deeds. You may remember how disappointed Jesus was once to find a fig-tree with plenty of leaves, but no fruit (Matthew 21. 18-20). He compared it to the Pharisees: plenty of talking about God, but very little living like Him. 'Why call ye Me, Lord, Lord,' He said to them, 'and do not the things which I say?' (Luke 6. 46). To profess to follow Christ, and yet not to do as He says, and live a life which is unworthy of Him, is to take the name of the Lord in vain. It is like a soldier who claims to belong to a crack regiment, but does nothing to maintain its traditions or advance its reputation, but rather the reverse. The good soldier of Jesus Christ is the one whose words are matched by deeds, and whose behaviour is a living advertisement of the faith which he claims to experience.

III—FAMILIARITY

'Familiarity breeds contempt,' runs the proverb, and contempt of God, His word and commandments, is a very dangerous state of mind. We need therefore to be very careful not to get into a flippant, familiar frame of mind where spiritual things are concerned. There is, of course, real humour in the Bible, and plenty of scope for laughter; but we must be very much on our guard against a light-hearted, jocular, easy-going approach to sacred things.

If we continually poke fun at or ridicule another person's possessions, his clothes, or car, or habits, we shall find that sooner or later, whether we mean to or not, we begin to lose any feeling of respect for the person himself. In the same way, if we treat the things which belong to God in a frivolous or flippant way, we shall find before long that we are looking upon God Himself with a little less awe and reverence than we should, or than He deserves.

Do you remember the story of Uzzah? (2 Samuel 6. 1-11). He was punished by God for touching, just touching, the ark. It seemed unfair at first sight, and David thought so, and indulged in an uncharacteristic piece of sulking. But looking at it more closely, we can see what must have happened. They were conveying this very sacred emblem, the ark, on a cart, and were obviously in a light-hearted mood, no doubt chatting and laughing, and probably travelling much too fast; for we read that the oxen stumbled, and the ark slipped. Uzzah steadied it with his hand and for this God punished him. His sin was to treat sacred things light-heartedly. In act, if not in word, he was taking the name of the Lord in vain.

Perhaps blasphemy and swearing are a temptation to those who have not had a particularly Christian upbringing. Familiarity is, I am sure, something which those who have enjoyed a Christian home need to be especially careful about. Long acquaintance with the Bible, Church services, hymns and prayers can produce this frivolous, superficial approach which is so dangerous; and once we begin to treat God with less reverence than He deserves, we are treating Him with contempt.

6. A DAY TO REMEMBER

THE Jewish Sabbath was a kind of national sign of their faith in God and their special relationship to Him, and it was most scrupulously observed. It had its roots in the Creation story, and was primarily intended to be a day of rest (Genesis 2. 1-3); but it became also a day of recollection, when the people gratefully remembered their deliverance from the land of Egypt (Deuteronomy 5. 12-15). After the coming of Christ, however, Christians realized that they had an even greater deliverance to commemorate in His death and resurrection from the grave, and it was felt that it would be more appropriate if the first day of the week was honoured rather than the last. In this way the Christian Sunday took the place of the Jewish Sabbath.

It is probably true to say that this commandment arouses more misunderstanding and is more widely disregarded than any other. People are prepared to admit that they should not kill or steal, however much they may be tempted to do so, but they question the very foundation of this commandment. In their view it is not even reasonable. 'Surely,' we hear them say, 'I can do what I like on Sunday. Why should I be bound by a whole lot of Old Testament rules? Why, even the day itself has been changed from the last day of the week to the first, apparently without divine permission, so why not the way in which it can be spent? And anyway, didn't Jesus say that "the Sabbath was made for man, and not man for the Sabbath?" ' (Mark 2. 27).

It must be admitted at the outset that this is a subject on which Christians themselves will very often agree to differ, because we cannot be certain to what extent the Christian Sunday inherited the rules and regulations governing the Jewish Sabbath. Not only do we find different standards adopted by Christians living in different parts of the world, but also the nature of Sunday observance has varied sharply throughout history, ever since it was first regulated by legislation in the Fourth Century; from the extreme strictness of the Seventeenth Century, when you were not even allowed to go for a walk, to the almost total liberty of today.

The observance of the Sabbath in Old Testament days was subject to the same fluctuations. At one extreme the people were warned by God to 'turn away ... from doing thy pleasure on My holy day' (Isaiah 58. 13); while at the other extreme they were reproved by Jesus for adding to the great principles which God had laid down a whole lot of tiresome, pettifogging little rules of their own. They reproached Jesus and His disciples for picking the ears of corn as they walked through the fields, and no doubt in their eyes it would have been a sin to pick a blackberry on your way back from church. The phrase which we sometimes use—'a Sabbath day's journey' —refers to the distance which a Jew was allowed to walk on that day. He could go 2,000 cubits or about seven miles, and no further.

Is it possible to find some way of preserving the

purpose of Sunday without making it unnecessarily burdensome? Can we enjoy it without violating the principles for which it was ordained? This is the problem that confronts us, and though in the last resort the individual Christian's conscience must be the final umpire in such a matter, I hope that what follows will help him to reach the right decision.

We are certainly safe in saying that no one will quarrel with the idea of one day's rest in seven. Indeed, on this matter the State has overtaken the Christian Church, and the five-day working week is generally accepted as a basic right. There have been attempts to work a ten-day week, but such practices defeat their own purpose, for they lead to absenteeism and falling output. The need for a regular time of rest is a fundamental law of nature, and God knew exactly what He was doing when He set aside one day each week for this purpose.

To this general rule of doing no work on Sundays, Jesus made three exceptions. First, there were *works of emergency*. He spoke of a farmer whose ox or ass fell into a pit (Luke 14. 5). Would he leave it there until Monday? Of course not! The animal must be rescued at once, even if it meant sending for the RSPCA or the local vet. I remember once, that we had to send for the fire brigade on a Sunday. It was regrettable, no doubt, and we disliked having to do it, but obviously inevitable in the circumstances. Exceptions of this sort are frequently occurring, especially in a country like Britain with such unpredictable weather. When a pipe bursts, or our dog is lost, we must do something about it immediately, and emergency operations are required.

Then there are *works of necessity*. In other words,

life must go on. It cannot come to a standstill one day every week. People must be fed and warmed, and the essential services must be maintained. If you are on board ship, you cannot expect the ship to spend the whole day in the doldrums just to meet the over-scrupulous conscience of some passenger. That is why Jesus allowed His disciples to pick the corn when they were hungry (Matthew 12. 1), and tried to show the Jews that the Sabbath was made for man, and not vice versa; and man would be unlikely to believe this if at the end of the day he found himself hungry, cold and uncared-for. It is clear, too, that Jesus included under this heading all work connected with public worship and the taking of services.

Again, there are *works of charity*. Think of the woman who came to Jesus to be healed on a Sunday (Luke 13. 16). 'Why can't you come back tomorrow?' asked the Jews. 'You've already waited eighteen years to be cured, and another twenty-four hours won't hurt you.' But Jesus did not see it like that at all. Why should Satan be allowed to spoil this woman's life for one moment longer than was necessary? Think of all the people who would go unhealed and unhelped if doctors, clergy, missionaries and teachers followed the advice of those Jews!

Sunday is an excellent day on which to do something useful and helpful. There are elderly people whom we can visit, or drive to church, or perhaps bring home to watch some programme on TV which they are specially anxious to see. There are sick people for whom we can do some household chore or to whom we can read. There is sure to be someone who will be encouraged and gratified to receive a letter from us on Monday morning; while there is almost certainly something we can find to do which will be a help to our local church. These are not breaches of the commandment, but opportunities to use the day positively and beneficially for the sake of others.

But these are exceptions. The general rule holds good. The chief purpose of Sunday is to give us the chance to rest from the books, the tools, the vehicles, the ledgers, money, bricks and the hundred and one other things which have engaged and absorbed our attention for the rest of the week. If we observe this rule, we shall come back to work on Monday refreshed and invigorated. If we do not observe it, we shall find that our work may very well become 'weary, stale, flat and unprofitable'.

But is there any reason why everyone should have the same day of rest? Why can't they have whichever day they like, and wouldn't some staggered arrangement be better? To some extent this happens already, but the great advantage of everyone as far as possible having the same day of rest is that we don't then make work for each other. The local librarian knows that there is no bus to get him to work on Sunday morning, but he doesn't worry, because he also knows that the library will be closed and there will be no customers.

But Sunday is not only a 'Rest Day', it is also 'The Lord's Day', for we read that God not only rested on the Sabbath Day, but sanctified it, or set it apart for Himself, as a day on which He was to be honoured and worshipped.

This means that on Sundays we shall try to give a little more time to God than we are able to do during the other six days. If we are lucky, there will be opportunities of meeting informally with other Christians, encouraging them, enjoying and benefitting from their company. Christian 'fellowship', as the New Testament calls it, when problems and ideas can be exchanged, discussed and prayed about together, is one of the most valuable experiences we can have, and one of the most fruitful means of spiritual growth.

As Christians too we ought to try to attend some form of Christian worship. There can be very few valid excuses, apart from illness, for missing church. I know how tired people can get. I know all about living in the country, a mile from the nearest church. But I honestly don't think these excuses carry very much weight. If we think of the trouble we take and the sacrifice we make to go to a football or cricket match, to see some show or visit some friend, we must admit that we often make very feeble excuses when it comes to church attendance.

For some I know it is much harder than for others, because there are homes where no one else goes to church, and you can only do so by disrupting a programme which takes no account of your own personal wishes. If you are faced with this sort of deadlock, then perhaps you may have to give way the first time with as good a grace as possible, but to ask that in future the time-table should be so arranged as to give you the chance to get to church some time during the course of the day. An imaginative and reasonable approach to the problem, if you can make it without appearing superior or sanctimonious, should achieve the desired result. If it does not do so, and you are faced with a clear-cut choice of going to church or doing what your parents ask, then while you are under age, you will probably feel that you ought to choose the latter.

But if we can become regular church-goers, then I am sure we should do so. We owe it to God to respect and reverence Him in this way. We owe it to other people who will be encouraged by our presence, or who may be tempted to follow our example if we are not there. We owe it to our minister and to our church; for who knows whether our attendance may not inspire him, and help forward the life of our church as a whole? We owe it to ourselves, for, when all is said and done, there is every chance that we shall learn something we did not know before, and that God will speak to us through the sermons, lessons, hymns and prayers, and send us on our way refreshed and encouraged.

It is an excellent habit, too, to try to spend a little longer on Sundays in prayer and Bible reading, and in studying the kind of books which will help us in our Christian lives; and there may be some meeting which we can attend in addition to church. But the great thing is to try to make Sunday the sort of day on which we give ourselves the chance to take firm and definite steps forward in the Christian life. The weekdays have been spent accumulating intellectual or financial wealth. Let Sunday be the day for acquiring spiritual wealth.

I have already mentioned some forms of Christian service, and this is the third way in which we can use Sunday positively, benefitting ourselves and other people, as well as honouring God. What we can do will, of course, vary with our age and circumstances. There may be, as I have suggested, visits we can pay, friends we can see, letters we can write. The chance may well come our way to take some active share in the life of our church. There is a tremendous need for voluntary Christian work of one sort or another, and every church in the country owes a great debt to men and women who are prepared to spend part of their Sunday helping in this way.

We have considered the two main purposes of Sunday—rest and worship or service, but obviously we cannot spend the whole day in bed or in church, and I am well aware that if we are going to achieve the sort of balance I spoke of earlier, there are several difficult problems which must be tackled.

'I would have thought that Sunday was designed for man to do exactly as he pleased'—so wrote a 15-year-old schoolboy to me on the very day I was beginning to prepare this chapter. I agree with this view if he is thinking of the fact that the previous six days have been spent trying to please those who teach him, and here is his chance to forget about his academic obligations; but I don't agree with it if he imagines that pleasing himself can ever be unconditional.

Let us consider some practical questions. '*My exams are coming up soon, and I want to spend a good part of Sunday studying my set books.*' I can see how this could be necessary, but before starting I would like to feel that the person concerned, whom I assume to be a Christian, had asked himself two questions.

First, will I fall a victim to the law of diminishing returns? In other words, may I achieve more by attempting less, and would a complete rest from work on Sunday stimulate me to apply myself more effectively throughout the coming week? Admittedly, this is a mental rather than a moral problem, but I think most working people would agree that it is the sounder principle to follow.

Secondly, will this work interfere with my chance to use Sunday in the positive, spiritual sort of way which I have suggested? I think if the choice had to be between the two, I would like to think that I could trust God not to allow success or failure in my exam to depend upon a few extra hours' work on Sunday. After all, we have His word, 'them that honour Me I will honour' (1 Samuel 2. 30).

'I get little chance to play games in the week, and very much want to keep part of Sunday free for some kind of sport.' What has just been said about a possible clash of loyalties applies perhaps with even greater force to sport than it does to work. We are faced in this case too with the whole thorny problem of Sunday games, and where, if at all, we ought as Christians to draw the line.

In his excellent paragraphs on this subject in *Parson's Pitch*, David Sheppard (the Bishop of Woolwich) distinguishes between what we do in private and taking part in organized and perhaps commercialized sport. I entirely agree. In the first case we are probably not involving others in work—car-park attendants, waitresses, stewards and so on—while in the second case we probably are; and I should hate to think that by indulging myself I was making it harder for others to go to church if they wanted to. But I think also that even in private we need to be careful, and must think what we are doing. If we are known to be practising Christians, then our family, our friends and our neighbours are going to watch us pretty closely, and someone might conclude that if I, a practising Christian, could give up a large part of Sunday to sport, then it is not such a sacred and important day after all. One of the problems of living the Christian life is that we so easily influence others. It is not enough that we do what is right; we must be seen to do it as well.

'I look forward to Sunday, because it gives me a little more time for my hobbies.' Of course, there are hobbies and hobbies. If people who are trying to rest are disturbed by our mowing machine or record-player, then for their sakes if for no other reason, we should refrain; but this would not apply to the many quieter hobbies which people can enjoy. Once again we need to be sure that it does not interfere with other and more important things, and to take care not to make Sunday a day of complete self-indulgence which we spend glued to the television, or to our record-player, favourite novel or newspaper. 'What spiritual progress have I made today?' is perhaps the first question we ought to ask ourselves as we go to bed on Sunday night.

. . . . . .

As I said at the outset, this whole question of Sunday observance is a very difficult one, partly because there has never been any clear consensus of Christian opinion on the subject, and each of us must carve out for himself the line he feels he ought to take. Precisely how we spend it, therefore, is up to us, but the purpose of the day is clear; and it will have failed in that purpose if at its close it does not find us physically rested, mentally refreshed and spiritually revived.

7. PARENTS AND SIMILAR PROBLEMS

I HOPE you won't be tempted to skip this chapter, because I am afraid the fifth commandment will oblige us to talk about the rather unpopular idea of authority; for out in the East, in Old Testament days, the words 'father' and 'mother' applied not only to parents, but to rulers, magistrates, schoolmasters and the like. This is not a very popular twentieth-century notion. Authority has become rather a dirty word, and there are many young people who do not like to feel that they owe any sort of submission to anyone.

Two things are worth saying at the outset. First, there must be submission to authority. If any society is to prosper and survive, whether it is a country, a town, a school or a home, the law-breaker and the hooligan cannot be allowed to get away with it. Secondly, this book is addressed to Christians. We cannot expect those who do not believe in Christ to accept His standards or try to follow His example; but if we do profess and call ourselves Christians, then it is worth noting how Jesus accepted authority. Although He was the Son of God, and needed no one to teach Him, yet He submitted Himself to His parents and to the leaders of His country and to the imperial authority of Rome. He obeyed laws, He paid taxes and He accepted the fact that 'the powers that be are ordained of God' (Romans 13. 1). Let us see how all this can apply to us:

I—CITIZENS

There can be no doubt that the Christian ought to be a law-abiding citizen, and submit himself 'to every institution for the sake of the Lord' (1 Peter 2. 13, 14). I know that there is a sense in which 'the law is an ass', as one of Dickens' characters says, and that there are hundreds of laws on the statute book which no one would dream of enforcing, and which are honoured more in the breach than the observance; but it is equally true that there are many laws which we know perfectly well that it is wrong to break, and when we do so we are aware that we are trying to get away with something that is illegal.

All this makes sense in a Christian country, but what if a government becomes utterly corrupt, and there seems to be no legal means of changing it? What ought a Christian to do then? Perhaps if he can do so he should leave the country, but otherwise I think he ought to try to work peaceably and within the law for the reforms he wants to see. The government of Rome was in many ways corrupt and evil, but there is no hint in the New Testament that it should be overthrown by force. In the end, the peaceful leaven of Christian influences prevailed, and this, it seems to me, is the only way in which policies which we detest should be changed. Violence is a short cut, and though at times the temptation to use it must be almost irresistible, it nearly always unleashes even greater evils than it seeks to remove. The film *Cromwell* brings out the reluctance with which that Christian man allowed himself to be drawn into the Great Rebellion, and one wonders whether peaceful means would not have proved more effective in the long run.

II—STUDENTS

Should a Christian obey the school or college rules? This is quite a serious problem for young people, and one which I have been asked about myself. There are, of course, two kinds of rule. There is one with a definite moral content, and there is the other sort which is made for convenience, and to give a proper order and pattern to life. About the first sort there can be no doubt at all. The Christian must take a firm stand on the side of law and order, and for what is right against what is wrong.

But what about the second kind? That admittedly is more difficult. Everyone knows that it adds spice to school life, for example, to run an occasional risk by breaking a rule, and no one thinks any the worse of the offender, least of all the person responsible for punishing him. Yet here, too, the Christian ought surely to set an example, and if he is constantly in trouble for breaking rules, he rapidly becomes a nuisance and a menace, and the effect of his Christian witness is seriously diminished. The desire to break rules usually comes from a spirit of adventure, but nowadays there is an increasing number of ways in which this can be exercised reasonably and legitimately.

And what are we to say about student marches, protests and demonstrations? A Christian may well feel that this is not just a worthy and effective but indeed the only possible way of drawing attention to a moral or social evil. If so, he will want to take part, but he will use his influence on the side of law and order, and try to keep the whole thing peaceful and good-humoured.

III—CHILDREN

When the Bible tells us to 'honour' our fathers and mothers, what exactly does it mean? I think we can say that this word has three meanings. First, it means that while we are still young our parents have a right to expect us to *obey* them. The right sort of parent will extract that obedience in a kind, loving and understanding way; and the right kind of child will gradually want to give it. But if there is to be any order or comfort in the home, obedience there must be. It has been my privilege to stay in the homes of any number of people in the last thirty years and I would certainly say that the happiest and best are those where this obedience is expected and given.

I could write at some length about the duty of parents to children; but that does not come into the fifth commandment, though the Bible has something to say about it elsewhere (Colossians 3. 21). There are parents who do not deserve the obedience of their children, either because they try to get it in the wrong way, or else because they ask for something a child has no right to give, the sacrifice of his conscience. But I am convinced that such cases are the exception, and that most parents approach this matter in the right spirit.

Of course, there comes a time in every family when parents have no longer the right to expect obedience, nor need children feel obliged to give it. Just when this comes depends upon many things. I think I would say that the right expires when children are no longer dependent upon their parents. The girl who is married, or the boy who has taken a job and is earning his own living, cannot be ordered about like children, and no sensible parents would try to do it.

But obedience is only of real value if we *respect* our parents as well. Obedience is the response we make to someone's command, but respect is the response that we make to their character, and will lead us to understand and appreciate the reasons and motives which lie behind the orders that are given. The Christian boy and girl whose parents ask them to be in the house by a certain hour, or not to go around with a certain person, will not fly off the handle, and start grumbling and sulking. They will try to see that their parents are not just wanting to exercise their authority, but are acting out of love, and doing what they honestly believe to be best for them.

Respect of this sort will outlast the time of actual obedience. We shall realize that, from their love and experience, our parents are able to give us the best possible advice. They know us better than anyone else does, and are in a position to guide and help us in many ways. If we are wise, we shall continue to benefit from their advice for as long as they are spared, even though we do not always follow it.

It is easy when we are young to think of our parents as being old-fashioned. We must remember that when they were young, they felt like that, so they should understand just what is going on in our minds. But do we want them to be up-to-date in quite that sense? Do we want them to dress as we do, and to share our taste in music and art? Part of the pleasure of having parents growing old is the fact that they see things rather differently from us. Their experience matches our enthusiasm. We see visions, while they dream dreams (Joel 2. 28).

But sometimes this respect is damaged and even destroyed because there is an almost total breakdown in communication between the generations. When this happens, the fault is very rarely all on one side, and for our part, we must do all we can to repair matters. But I think that it is very often here that the advice and help of an older friend can be of such value. Within the Church of England, for example, it is ideally the task of godparents to interpret children to parents and vice versa. But where they are not available or suitable, there is usually someone who shares the confidence of both sides. 'The old man isn't being deliberately obstructive, you know', 'The girl isn't doing it just to annoy you'—this sort of mediation by someone whom everybody respects can be an enormous help.

To obey, to respect, and, best of all, to *love*. This is the deepest side of our relationship to them, and it is from this that obedience and respect will grow. It is as we realize that they have done much and perhaps sacrificed much for us that we shall love them in return. We tend to take for granted what our parents do for us. Perhaps up to a point it is well that we should. It is, after all, a sign of our trust in them. But as time goes on it should blossom into more conscious love.

Later on, the chance may come to show our love in a practical way. As our parents grow old, and perhaps infirm, they often tend to look towards us for support and sympathy. This is one way in which we can show our gratitude to them for all that they have done for us. Another way, which can present itself, is by never being ashamed of them. Many young people today are enjoying a far better start in life than their parents had. It is very easy for them to grow a little proud, and slightly ashamed of their parents. Book knowledge, influential friends, a polished accent, the right clothes—all these are things which can come between parents and children. To grow too grand for your parents is the worst possible kind of snobbery, especially when it is remembered that it may have been the father's generosity and the mother's sacrifice which provided these advantages in the first place.

Finally, love for our parents will express itself in prayer. Probably for most of us the first prayer we ever uttered was 'God bless mummy and daddy . . .'. As time goes on we begin to do a bit better than that, and to remember before God their problems, their work, and so on. And if perhaps they are not true Christians in the sense we understand, and do not know or love the Lord Jesus Christ, then we can pray that they may come to do so; and there have been many cases where Christian children have been the means of winning their own parents for Christ. Their prayers, their quiet witness and example, some book, perhaps, which they have lent, or a word here or there, and before long a father or mother has shared the faith of their children, and discovered in Jesus Christ the same Saviour, Friend and Guide. And this in its turn creates a deeper relationship still; for love for our parents in the Christian sense is only complete when we share with them our faith in Jesus Christ.

I must deal lastly with one problem which we cannot, unfortunately, escape. It is the problem of the unhappy and the divided home. All that I have said about obedience, respect and love applies to the home which I hope most readers enjoy, and I certainly did; but what about the home where the father and mother do not hit it off, where there is quarrelling, bickering and friction, maybe ending in separation and divorce? What are we to do then?

I have observed that it is very rarely the case that one party is wholly to blame. There are usually faults on both sides, and it takes two to make a quarrel. I have talked with couples who have fallen out. I listen to the husband, and I think I have heard the whole story. Then I meet the wife—and what a different tale! What is one to believe? Simply that while one party may be very much more to blame, there is something to be said on the other side.

This leads me to say to young people who are faced with this problem that it is best to try not to take sides. Try as far as you can to be fair to both, impartial in your attitude, and equally loving and obedient. Very often parents refuse to separate and divorce (and all honour to them) for the sake of the children. Therefore you may be the one link which is holding them together. You are in fact in a position of great strength and influence, and you can show them that their decision to stay together for your sake has been justified, that you appreciate what they have done, and that by your love and humility you are anxious to heal the breach.

If it finally comes to separation and divorce, then, I am afraid, if you are under age, the decision as to where you live is taken out of your hands. One parent (usually the mother) is granted custody and the other access, the right to see you from time to time. As you get older, you may have to make up your mind to throw your lot in completely with one or the other, but while you are still young, and dependent upon them, you want to try to maintain your neutrality. You may find that one parent attempts to enlist your sympathy and support against the other, but unless you are very sure where the great weight of blame lies, it is better not to be drawn in this way. Give to both, as far as you can, your love and affection, and try to remember that but for the fact that they once loved each other, you wouldn't be here at all.

8. IF LOOKS COULD KILL...

Four of the most precious things that people possess are their life, their wife (or husband), their property and their reputation; and the next four commandments have been designed to protect these. There may even be something in the order chosen, because man's most precious possession is his life, and to take the life of another person is still regarded as the most serious offence there is.

Although this commandment says, 'Thou shalt not kill', it is clear that it is aimed at what we now call murder, the wilful, deliberate extinction of life. Very early in the Bible we find a distinction made between murder and manslaughter (Exodus 21. 12, 13). There were special legal provisions to protect the man who killed someone else by accident or in self-defence. The law, both then and now, does not look upon these as murder.

Probably all of us breathe a sigh of relief when we reach this commandment. We can think of many occasions when we have broken the first five, but we can confidently plead 'Not Guilty' to Number 6. We all agree that murder is utterly wrong, and for the murderer we reserve the very severest penalties.

But Jesus doesn't let people get away with it quite as easily as that. He took great trouble, you remember, not only to condemn murder, but also the poisonous roots from which it sprang. This is an example, in fact, of the way in which He 'fulfilled' the law. He showed that the act of murder was just that part of the iceberg which appears above the surface, and He levelled His attack against the seven-eighths which lay beneath. There are in fact three chief causes of murder, three ways, if you like, in which we may murder someone with our minds, our looks, or our tongues long before we actually lay hands upon them.

I—ANGER

Many acts of violence are the result of a sudden, uncontrollable loss of temper. A wave of anger comes over a man, and before he knows what is happening, he has done something which he will for ever after regret. Most of us have probably been aware at times of such surgings within us which make us want to strike a person. We are provoked to the point at which we can stand it no longer, and we lash out with our tongues and even our fists.

It is a very sobering thought that within each one of us there lurks this tiger which we call temper. For a great deal of the time it lies dormant, and gives little hint of its presence or power. Then something stirs it, and before we know where we are, it has broken loose, and is doing any amount of damage.

None of us is free from this temptation, although in some of us the urge seems to be stronger than in others. The best of us needs to be on our guard against these surprise outbreaks. You may be one of those people who finds it very hard to argue with anyone without losing his temper. Perhaps it is a political discussion. It starts calmly enough, and then the argument gets a bit heated, fur begins to fly, angry words are spoken, and even blows exchanged. Or is your difficulty concerned with games? You take them very keenly, you hate losing, and are desperately anxious to win. Things are at fever pitch, and the decision is given against you—'fault', 'offside', 'out'. It is the last straw. You don't want to let fly, but you are off your guard, and there is a furious display of bad temper. Or perhaps you are one of those who hate having their legs pulled. You put up with it for a bit, and then someone goes a bit too far in trying to take the micky out of you. He pokes the tiger in the eye . . .

Of course I know that it is probably only once in a million times that anger or loss of temper actually leads to murder. But it has done so, and it could do so again. We need therefore to be constantly on our guard. It is rather like small-pox. Only very rarely now does anyone die of it, but that does not mean we can relax our precautions, or stop vaccinating babies. So by prayer and vigilance we need to protect ourselves, remembering that even a display of anger is unworthy of a true follower of Jesus Christ (Matthew 5. 21, 22).

II—HATRED

Another very common ancestor of murder is hatred. It is possible to get such a settled dislike of another person that we find it almost impossible to speak decently to him. 'I can't stand the person,' we say. Of course, we never get round to thinking about murder, even though we may say, 'I wish you were dead'; but that is not the point. The point is that it *could* lead to murder, and has done so in many cases, and that if murder is wrong, then the things that give rise to it are wrong too.

Of course, we cannot like everyone. It is natural for us to feel drawn to some people and repelled by others. But Jesus tried to teach us to love our enemies (Matthew 5. 43, 44). That does not mean that we shall suddenly find we like John Brown better than we used to do, but it does mean that our attitude towards him can change. Instead of 'wishing him dead', we shall look for secret ways of doing him a good turn. We shall pray for him, and try to break down the barrier of dislike which has been built up between us. The curious thing is that we shall begin to find that our feelings about him change, that we no longer hate him, and that he is 'not nearly as bad as I thought'.

III—ENVY

Perhaps this is the most subtle and dangerous of all the roots which lie beneath murder. My garden suffers from a most pernicious weed called 'ground elder'. Now and then I attack it for all I am worth. I pull it up, I poison it, I smother it with other plants; but it is no good. Year after year it goes on growing beneath the surface, and the experts tell me that the only thing to do is to dig it right out and start again.

Envy is like that. It works underground, sometimes for years, and then suddenly breaks out in the shape of some bitter, disgraceful word, or letter, or action. Very often we do not know what a grip it has got upon the garden of our lives until it is given some favourable opportunity to show itself. The *first* murder in the Bible was the result of envy. Do you recall the occasion? Cain and Abel both brought offerings to God, and while God was delighted with Abel's, He had no respect for Cain's. We will not bother to go into the reason for this, but the result was that Cain got furiously jealous of his brother, and took the first opportunity of putting him to death (Genesis 4. 1-15). And the *worst* murder in the Bible was also the result of envy; for you will remember that it was 'for envy' that the Jews delivered Jesus to be crucified (Matthew 27. 18). How true it is that 'envy is a sharper spur than pay'!

Envy takes various forms. We can envy other people their success, their looks, their popularity, their ease of manner and charm. Sometimes our envy can take a more concrete form. We want another person's possessions or position, or property or friend. We shall deal with this more fully when we think about the tenth commandment—'Thou shalt not covet', but at this stage it is worth noting that envy itself really grows from pride. It is because we want to be richer, more successful, more famous, or whatever it is, that we are envious of other people who are.

Perhaps the most effective poison for envy is humility. The kind of person in whose life envy finds it very hard to grow is the kind of person who has learnt to think of himself modestly and sensibly. He has learned to accept the fact that he is poorer, uglier, less intelligent or athletic than other people he knows. It has been said that there are two kinds of humility; learning to succeed without conceit, and learning to fail without complaint. The person who can do that is the truly humble person. He won't give envy a chance.

· · · · · ·

We cannot leave this subject without touching quite briefly on some rather special instances of killing about which we ought to know the Christian attitude, if there is one. A great deal has been written about them, and it is right that Christians should give them thought.

I—SUICIDE

Is it ever right for a man to take his own life? There is, usually, a difference between *taking* our life and *giving* it. A man like Captain Oates, 'the very gallant gentleman' of Scott's last expedition, walked out of the tent to his death in order to give his friends a better chance of survival. We can have nothing but praise for him, or for the millions of men and women who have given their lives for their country, or in some great cause. Did not Jesus Himself say, 'Greater love hath no man than this, that a man lay down his life for his friends'? (John 15. 13).

Suicide is different, and is universally condemned by Christians. There are no doubt circumstances, perhaps when a country is at war, when a man will take his own life rather than risk torture and the possible betrayal of vital secrets to the enemy; and during the last war men who were known to be on Hitler's black list carried cyanide tablets in their pockets. This is rather different, and really amounts to 'giving' rather than 'taking' your own life. But in the ordinary way suicide is wholly un-Christian. It is God who has given us our lives, and it is for Him to take them away in His own time.

Suicide is usually committed by people the balance of whose minds are disturbed, or who find themselves in a situation which they lack the courage or the capacity to face; and it is a form of escape from life which no one need even contemplate for a moment who has God as his 'refuge and strength' (Psalm 46. 1).

II—MERCY KILLING

This is the usual description of 'euthanasia', the deliberate taking of someone's life when a doctor has described the person's condition as incurable. Here is a woman dying of cancer, suffering acutely. Is there any point in prolonging her pain and discomfort for a few more weeks or months?

Christians believe that we are in God's hands, and that we ought not to usurp His prerogative of taking away life at the moment when it seems best to Him. It may be that He still has something He wants to teach the patient through his or her suffering. It could be that those who watch, inspired by the faith of the sufferer, will be drawn more closely to Him. 'His illness and death converted one of his doctors', wrote a mother to me recently about her twenty-year-old son who had just died of leukaemia. It could be that it is still His purpose to work some apparently miraculous cure. We dare not rule out the possibility.

III—CAPITAL PUNISHMENT

This is a subject on which Christians differ sharply. Some believe that because the death penalty was imposed in the Old Testament on the grounds that the murderer was really assaulting the life of God (Genesis 9. 6), and was accepted in the New (Luke 23. 41. Acts 25. 11), it should be regarded as a permanent institution. They regard it moreover as the only way of protecting the good name of society and expressing its condemnation of the crime of murder and of deterring others who may be thinking of doing the same.

Others will argue that, just as it has been abolished for lesser crimes, so we have reached a point at which it should be abolished for murder. They maintain that its value as a deterrent is questionable, that every punishment must be remedial and seek to reform the criminal, and that if there is a miscarriage of justice or fresh evidence comes to light afterwards, it is too late to do anything about it.

Perhaps that is as far as you can take the argument, realizing that in a fallen and sinful world there are many subjects on which we shall be unable to find the perfect answer with which all Christians will agree.

IV—WAR

And here I believe is another problem to which there is not, and perhaps there never can be, a final Christian answer. Should a Christian fight? This became a particularly burning issue during the last war. There were many who were convinced that it was quite wrong for them in any circumstances to take up arms against other people. In World War I such 'conscientious objectors', as they were called, were imprisoned. In World War II, provided they could convince a tribunal that their convictions were sincere, they were allowed to work on the land, in hospitals, and in other ways; and many of them did most gallant and useful work.

This change of attitude towards pacifists between

1919 and 1939 was perhaps due to the fact that the authorities realized that freedom of conscience was one of the chief things the war was being fought about. It hardly made sense to lock up your own pacifists in prison and at the same time fight for the right to believe and act as your conscience told you to do. A much more tolerant attitude developed. People realized that the problem was not as simple as they had imagined, and that the conscientious objector had a good case to make out. How right was he, and how far ought Christians today to reject war as the ultimate method of settling international controversy?

The problem arises from the fact that we are trying to apply Christian standards and ideals in a world where they will not fit. If everyone had abstained from fighting in 1939-45, the Nazis would have overrun Europe and imposed on all the subjugated peoples an utterly unchristian and amoral system of government and way of life. Should we have submitted to another 'Dark Ages', confident in the belief that God's purposes would one day prevail? Or was it better to fight the war, with its fearful loss of life, to prevent the eclipse of civilisations, perhaps for generations to come?

It is my own firm belief that it was, and that the New Testament, while condemning violence as a way of settling personal disputes, cannot be held to apply the same rule on an international level. But you notice that while I say that it was the 'better' decision, I do not say it was right. It was the choice between two evils—the awful evil of war, and the even greater evil, as I feel it to be, of cultural and spiritual extermination.

It is on those same grounds that I personally believe that we should retain the nuclear deterrent. It is a hideous weapon, but I think it can be argued that it may prevent war, and thereby save civilization. But while I hold these views, I know that a great many very good Christians believe just the opposite, and the important thing is that we should agree to differ in sincerity and love.

V—ABORTION

Is abortion a form of unlawful killing? Roman Catholics would say 'Yes', because they believe that from the moment of conception the foetus or unborn child is a living soul. Most other Christians would disagree, maintaining that life begins at birth, and that it is only at that point that we can speak of a new, separate and individual person.

This being so, it is argued that there are circumstances in which a pregnancy ought to be terminated, and the law in some countries, including Great Britain, has been amended to take account of these. It is now felt to be right and proper to allow abortions where a pregnancy is the result of rape, where it might result in the birth of a deformed or mentally defective child, where it could endanger the life of the mother, or her mental or physical health, or where her capacity to bring up an additional child was in serious doubt.

The fact that it was through the influence of Christianity that infanticide and abortion, so commonly practised in the past, were condemned and made illegal, has naturally made Christians cautious in their attitude towards changes in the law and anxious to make sure that these are not abused. Reluctantly they accept that in some circumstances abortion is the lesser of two evils, at the same time respecting those who feel that in a given situation nature should be allowed to take its course, and that the grace of God can be trusted to triumph even in the most unpromising circumstances.

9. HAPPILY EVER AFTER

ADULTERY is the word used to describe sexual intercourse between two people, either of whom is married to someone else. It is a practice which is condemned throughout the Bible, and yet it is terribly common, in our own country and throughout the world.

The kind of thing that happens is this. Two people marry, and for a time all goes well. Then their love for each other begins to cool, their physical attraction to wane, and one or other of them starts to look for satisfaction elsewhere. Sooner or later another man or woman turns up, and there is created what has been called 'the eternal triangle'.

A and B marry and have children. Then they quarrel, or simply get bored with each other. At the critical moment B meets C, falls in love, and enjoys sexual intercourse. A then decides to divorce B, partly because it seems the only thing to do, partly because B wants it this way, and partly perhaps because by this time D has appeared on the scene, and promises to be a very attractive substitute for B. So B and C marry, and then A and D, and we are left with this tragic little equation: $(A+D)(B+C) =$ a wrecked marriage + a broken home. Variations on this theme are almost limitless in number, and form the subject of some of the most popular novels, films and plays.

'But,' protests someone, 'why is it wrong? Why shouldn't people follow their inclinations? If the first marriage was a mistake, entered into too hastily, perhaps, then why must the couple live for ever in misery when all the time happiness is waiting for them just round the corner in the person of some other man and woman? Surely it is much better to cut your losses and start all over again? The chances of making the same mistake twice are greatly reduced, and there are thousands of very happy marriages which have emerged from this sort of chaos.'

I know. Put like that it does sound different. People caught up in this sort of tangled situation deserve our deepest sympathy and understanding, and there are many cases which work out much more happily than was feared at first. But we cannot escape the fact that adultery is condemned in the Bible as a sin. The reasons for it may be overwhelmingly plausible, and the results of it may be surprisingly successful; but no Christian can possibly believe that the act of adultery itself is right. It is a plain breach of the seventh commandment. And once again we can show that this commandment is natural and reasonable. When God says, 'Thou shalt not commit adultery', He is not being capricious. He is not just blocking up one more avenue to personal enjoyment, but is forbidding something which for at least three reasons is personally and socially harmful.

First, it can have a very disruptive effect on family life. Someone has said that the family is older than the church. From earliest times it has been God's purpose that one man and one woman should live together, and that their love for each other should form the foundation of a home for their children—the father, if you like, constituting the head and the mother the heart of that home (Genesis 2. 24. Matthew 19. 3-9). Adultery completely wrecks that. It destroys a unity which God means to be permanent. It removes from the home by the most drastic amputation either the head or the heart. It can leave children forlorn and rudderless, and they often take a long time to recover from the harmful effect of being deprived in this way of a father or mother.

I know, of course, that there are many cases where a single or an occasional act of adultery has not led to the collapse of the home. There has been repentance, forgiveness, reconciliation, and the home has recovered. But it is bound to shake the confidence which one partner of the marriage has in the other, and in any case sin can never be justified on the grounds that the person we are injuring will understand and forgive.

Secondly, it cuts at the roots of social confidence and integrity. There are many people who would never dream of stealing money from their neighbours, and yet have no hesitation about stealing the wife of a friend. But where is the difference? Is a man's silver more precious than his wife? And it is equally dishonourable for the wife to agree; for in a marriage neither partner has the right to give away to someone else what they have exclusively and permanently pledged to each other in the most solemn manner possible.

Thirdly, it makes enjoyment of the physical side of sex an end in itself. Sexual intercourse is only one of several reasons for marriage, and by itself alone it can never justify that tremendous step. What adultery does is to take sexual intercourse out of the context of marriage, and turn it into something to be sought and enjoyed for its own sake. It is rather the same as gluttony. We eat to live, we do not live to eat. A man who just eats for the sake of doing so, regardless of his need for food at any given moment, is a glutton. He degrades himself. In the same way men and women who enjoy sexual intercourse outside marriage, are simply indulging an appetite, and degrading themselves. The sex act is the consummation of marriage, the coping stone, not the foundation stone; and adultery turns the whole thing upside down.

. . . . . .

There are many people who deplore adultery, with its disruptive effect on the life of the home, and yet see nothing wrong with fornication, that is, sexual intercourse between two unmarried people. The argument runs like this: boys and girls are sexually mature many years before their social and economic circumstances make marriage possible. Is it therefore unreasonable that they should anticipate, with proper safeguards, some of the pleasures which marriage has in store for them? Moreover, by indulging themselves in this way they will be tasting life to the full, and living as we are in such uncertain and clouded days, can they be blamed for seizing opportunities as they come? And in any case, will not experience be valuable? Are they not more rather than less likely to settle down to a happy and permanent marriage if they have done a little experimenting first? They are faced on every hand by the breakdown of marriage, and they feel that anything which would minimize the risk of failure is to be welcomed.

When we add to these apparently reasonable arguments the fact that so many books, films, plays and even the advice of friends represent the experience as exceedingly desirable, is it to be wondered at that many young people take the line of least resistance, and follow the course dictated by instinct and by nature?

It must be said at the outset that, although it is not actually mentioned in the seventh commandment, fornication (that is, sexual intercourse of any sort outside marriage) like adultery, is emphatically forbidden in the Bible (1 Corinthians 6. 18). Jesus linked the two together, and they are as closely related as theft and robbery. This ought to be a good enough reason for the Christian to follow Paul's advice and 'flee fornication' (Ephesians 5. 3); but it may be helpful to see why to obey this command is reasonable as well as right.

First of all, there is still the risk, despite contraceptives and widespread abortion, of producing an unwanted baby, and adding to a social problem which is already acute; and even if the young people concerned satisfy themselves on this point, they are setting an example and encouraging a trend.

Secondly, just as there can be no true marriage without sexual intercourse, so sexual intercourse is regarded in the Bible as creating a union (1 Corinthians 6. 16) which can only be expressed in the larger union of marriage. As C. S. Lewis says, 'those who indulge in sexual intercourse outside marriage are trying to isolate one kind of union (the sexual) from all other kinds of union which were intended to go along with it and make up the total union.'

Thirdly, we must face the fact that fornication can

leave a permanent scar on someone's personality. What one partner may shrug off light-heartedly as of little account, the other, perhaps more introspective by nature, may look back upon with bitter regret, feeling that he (or she) can never be the same again. This is what Paul means when he says, 'the fornicator sins against his own body' (1 Corinthians 6. 18), and we must bear in mind that the word 'body' in the Bible includes our psychological as well as our physical make-up.

Fourthly, if we can learn, while we are still young, to harness and control our instincts, and finally to direct them aright, we are giving ourselves the greatest possible experience in self-discipline. A boy or a girl who has fought and won this particular battle has gained something of great value. They have made victory over lesser temptations much more likely. They have forearmed themselves against later sexual temptations from which even marriage will not bring immunity; for chastity before marriage is more and not less likely to produce faithfulness after marriage. They have also begun to forge that most valuable of all human possessions—a perfectly educated will.

Before we leave this discussion, there is perhaps one special case which we must consider. It concerns the young couple who are engaged to be married, but perhaps faced with a very long engagement. Is there any reason why they should not pick some of the fruits of marriage before the actual wedding-day? A good deal of what has already been said applies to this case as well as to any other; but perhaps two things might be added. First, an engagement does not guarantee marriage. From time to time engagements are broken off, quite honourably and sensibly, and the fact that this could happen really disqualifies this case from any special consideration. Secondly, the young couple probably look forward to being married in church, when they will ask God to create and bless their union. Would it not make rather a mockery of that service if they had already taken the law into their own hands by anticipating His sanction and blessing? As children we can perhaps remember asking for the birthday or Christmas present in advance, before the actual day. But a wise father or mother probably refused, wanting to teach us self-control, and feeling also that the day itself might lose something of its lustre and freshness and, if we may use the word, its mystery if we were given beforehand what was really meant to be its crowning happiness. That is rather the way in which the Christian imagines God to feel about marriage.

. . . . .

Some may feel that this is a terribly high standard. 'Granted,' they say, 'it may be the right one, but however can we live up to it, either before or after marriage?' Let me end this chapter therefore with a number of practical suggestions.

We must remember that all temptation begins with the thoughts. The thought, fostered and encouraged, will grow into the imagination, and that in turn into the desire. Therefore it is in the mind that the first battle must be fought and won. If we want victory, we must be sensible. We must guard the avenues through which temptation can invade our minds, and avoid the sort of situations and activities which will arouse our sexual passions and make their control more difficult. This is what Jesus meant when He said, 'If your right eye causes you to sin, take it out and throw it away!' (Matthew 5. 27-29).

Next comes this matter of friendship with those of the opposite sex—boy-friends or girl-friends, as the case may be. What should be said about them? Obviously the more we can meet them, in the context of our ordinary, everyday life, the better; and our attitude should be perfectly friendly in a natural, general sort of way. But perhaps we want to be careful if we find ourselves developing a friendship with one person to the exclusion of others at a time when we cannot even dream of engagement or marriage. Apart from the possible dangers we have already considered, this can be a distraction from work and other duties.

Again we must always recognize the fact that hugging, kissing and petting are not simply ways of expressing our feelings, they are also ways of stimulating our sexual desires; and as the ultimate danger is only reached by way of these well-marked milestones, we need to be particularly on our guard in this respect.

It is a very good idea to begin to pray about the person whom you will one day marry, if that is God's will. Somewhere that partner is waiting, and you must believe that step by step, in His own time and way, God will bring you together. That is why, for a Christian, all this talk about 'experimenting' is such nonsense. We believe that for every life God has a perfect plan which He wants to bring to pass (Romans 8. 28). If that plan for us includes marriage, then we can trust Him to bring it about without any clumsy and fumbling attempts on our part to help Him. Nothing convinces me more powerfully of the truth of this than the experience of my innumerable Christian friends and contemporaries. The happiness and success of their marriages have been due, I am sure, to this prayerful and spiritual approach.

These standards are high, and they may seem hard to reach, but the Christian is not expected to rely upon his own strength. Left to ourselves, we might easily fall, and grow discouraged; but we can do all things through the power of Christ (Philippians 4. 13). And that power we can harness to our own lives by things like prayer, Bible-reading, worship and the friendship of other Christians. In this way we can be what the Bible calls 'more than conquerors' (Romans 8. 37) of our temptations. We shall not just scrape through by the skin of our teeth, hard-pressed and exhausted, but we shall learn and benefit from every battle which we fight and win.

There are some young people who feel that if they fail in this area of their lives, they have somehow committed the unpardonable sin, and put themselves out of range of God's forgiveness. Nothing could be farther from the truth. God's mercy can reach 'to the uttermost' (Hebrews 7. 25) of man's need, and while adultery and fornication can involve others as well as ourselves in regrettable consequences, in God's sight they are no worse than any other sin.

When a woman who had been caught in the act of adultery was brought before Jesus, her accusers hoped that He would condemn her in scalding terms (John 8. 1-11), but He stooped down and began to write with His finger on the ground. One tradition tells us that He wrote the sins of which the accusers themselves were guilty, and when they began to read words like pride, jealousy and hypocrisy, one by one they slunk away from His presence. A self-righteous hypocrite who goes regularly to church may be nearer hell than a generous-minded prostitute.

10. A THEFT BY ANY OTHER NAME

'I AM firm, you are stubborn, he is pig-headed.' I remember reading that once, and it illustrated to me how easy it is to excuse faults which we see in ourselves, and condemn the same faults in other people. What looks like tiresome pig-headedness in the man next door is firmness of spirit in us. We can almost persuade ourselves that what is a vice in him is a virtue in us; and this is a dangerous state of mind.

But I believe it shows itself nowhere more clearly than in this matter of personal honesty. We are very quick to spot and pounce upon dishonesty in other people, but apt to overlook it or explain it away in ourselves. Apart from professional thieves, burglars and pickpockets, who make a living out of stealing other people's property, most people are appalled at the idea of taking what is not theirs with the deliberate intention of keeping it. What belongs to someone else is in a sense sacred, and we feel we cannot touch it without burning our fingers. In fact, this eighth commandment is one on which we feel we may be able to make up lost ground. We may not be too hot at Sunday observance, but to steal something which does not belong to us . . .

But that is just where we are apt to go wrong. Stealing is the supreme example of dishonesty, but it has a great many first cousins; and it is these which we are inclined to entertain quite happily, never considering for a moment that they are so closely related to such a despicable creature. What we must do now is to turn the pages of the family photograph album, and try to see the likeness and connection between theft on the one hand and its relations on the other.

I—DEFRAUDING

There are many people who would never dream of taking what does not belong to them, and yet are perfectly prepared to try to enjoy something without paying the proper price. Travelling without a railway ticket is perhaps the commonest example of what I mean. It has become a kind of adventure. Your wits are pitted against those of the inspector, and you hope that you will get away with it. If you do, you will have saved quite a bit of money; if you don't, well, that's too bad. And so each year the railways lose thousands of pounds, and the deficit has to be made up by making the innocent people pay more.

Then there are those who show you with great pride something which they have been able to slip past the customs without paying duty. Here again they find a nice glossy word for it. They call it a 'game'. So is poaching, I suppose, or thieving, in that if you get caught you pay, and if you do not get caught then someone else pays. People look very offended if you suggest that what they are really doing is smuggling. It is not a very pretty word. When you come to think about it, it is not a very accurate word either; the proper definition for this practice is stealing.

Again, it is quite easy to defraud the Inland Revenue of their rightful tax by making a false return, or by failing to declare every source of income. A High Court judge has said that no one is obliged to organize his tax affairs so as to give the advantage to the authorities nor does the Law usually concern itself with trifles. But at the same time, the Christian's conscience ought not to allow him to try to get away with a deliberate fiddle; and I sympathize with the Christian woman who wrote to me recently because she was worried about the money her husband was earning while he was drawing unemployment benefit.

Has it ever occurred to you that slackness over the payment of bills is really dishonest, and a way of defrauding a shopkeeper or tradesman? The money we owe ought to be earning interest for him, but instead of that it is lining our own pockets. I remember a Christian outfitter telling me once how hard he found it to get his accounts settled, even by some so-called Christians, and I made up my mind then and there to try not to offend in this way.

II—CHEATING

Money is not the only thing people steal. Very often, when young, we find that marks are more valuable, and it is important to get as many as we can. Things may have changed since I was at school, but I can remember that in the lower forms particularly, there were several ways of 'getting' rather than 'earning' marks. You could use what was called a 'crib', or you could copy the work of the person next door; and there were other devices as well.

Everyone knows that the 'cheat' in the end does himself no good, and is found out when the examinations come round. Marks are only incidental. The important thing is the development of the mind and the growth of knowledge. But this can never come if we adopt a 'get rich quickly' attitude towards our work in the class-room. It is always the result of industry and self-application.

It is also perfectly possible to cheat in other ways—in games, business, art and so on. Cheating in fact is everything which uses unfair means of depriving another person of the position, reputation or reward which he deserves to enjoy. As such it is often more profitable and less detectable than actual stealing. As Arthur Hugh Clough reminds us:

'Thou shalt not steal; an empty feat
When it's more lucrative to cheat.'

III—FINDING

'Finding's keeping,' an old saying goes; but there is only one place where, so far as I know, that rule applies—on the golf course! How pleasant it is, having driven an old ball into the middle of next week, to find, after a desultory search, a brand new one nestling in the heather, waiting for another owner! But that pound note you found on the sands last summer ought to have been taken to the police station. If at the end of three months no one had asked for it, I think you could have claimed it yourself. That is the law. We cannot just walk off with an umbrella which someone else has left in the train. We must take it to the lost property office.

IV—BORROWING

What sort of a borrower are you? I can think of three kinds. First, there is the person who borrows without asking. He is in a desperate hurry to get somewhere, and his bicycle has a flat tyre, so he 'borrows' the one next to it in the rack. Meanwhile the rightful owner turns up, finds it is missing, looks for it everywhere, and finally reports it as having been—borrowed?—No! *stolen!*

Then there is the forgetful borrower. He does at least ask if he may borrow the book, mackintosh, tennis racquet, or whatever it is, but he completely forgets to give it back. The poor owner either has to struggle along as best he can without his possession, or seek out the borrower who, as likely as not, has by this time forgotten where it is.

Finally, there is the person who borrows something, and then loses it—or damages or spoils it in some way, and returns it without getting it repaired, and often without apology or explanation. The disappointed owner finds his tennis racquet has been returned all right, but scratched and dirty; the dent on his front mudguard is never explained; and the grease marks on the cover of his book are a disappointing reminder of the thoughtless behaviour of his friend.

We need, I believe, to be particularly careful over the matter of borrowing money. A person hates to go on reminding his friend that he owes him 50p, and it is up to the borrower to repay his debt at the first opportunity, and to 'owe no man anything' (Romans 13. 8), as Paul said. I remember learning another lesson once. You may be the treasurer of various funds. There comes a time when you are short of cash, and feel it would be all right to borrow from one of the cash boxes. I make it a rule now always to put in an IOU with the date. Otherwise I might so very easily forget; or I might die before I could repay the debt, and my biographer would have some awkward explaining to do.

V—WASTING

It is terribly easy to waste time. We all find that. It is human nature to relax when given the chance to do so. This need not matter very much if the time is our own; but very often it is not. It has nearly always been paid for by someone else—our firm, our boss or our parents. Therefore if we waste what is not ours, whether money or what money will buy, we are strictly speaking guilty of stealing. In the same way it is fatally easy to be careless, extravagant and even dishonest with the use of the 'firm's' stationery, telephone, fuel and so on. The phrase, 'Don't worry, it is on the firm', is a dangerously pernicious one. It can colour our whole attitude towards things which we don't actually have to pay for ourselves, and it can lead to all kinds of misappropriation.

. . . . . .

When we thought about murder, we looked at some of the things which gave rise to it, and we discovered three principal ancestors—anger, malice and envy. Can we in the same way trace theft back to any particular source? Has it roots of its own? What makes a person want to steal and cheat?

I think it is fair to say that one of the reasons is *boredom*. Many people live in very drab surroundings, and they are working at a job which gives little scope for imagination or variety. Sometimes they must long for excitement and adventure, and there is no doubt that these things can be provided by pitting one's wits against the law. People today are very much aware of this problem, and it is up to those in authority to try to provide an increasing amount of profitable activity for those with an increasing amount of leisure.

Another reason is *laziness*. This seems to contradict what has just been said, but I don't think it does. The really industrious, hard-working person is rarely dishonest. Fraud and theft and things like that are a way of cutting corners, of getting things on the cheap, of growing rich without personal effort. Boys or girls, for example, who cheat at work are simply trying to save themselves trouble—the trouble and time they want to spend in what they feel to be more interesting pursuits.

Finally, there is *covetousness*. We will not deal with this at length, because the tenth commandment is devoted entirely to this one thing, But, in a word, it is this acquisitive spirit, this desire to possess what others have got and we lack, this 'something for nothing' approach to life, which leads many people into different forms of dishonesty. It is certainly true to say that if everyone obeyed the tenth commandment, a great many more would obey the eighth without even thinking about it.

11. THE TRUTH, THE WHOLE TRUTH...

THIS chapter finds us back again with the tongue. The third commandment warned us against taking God's name in vain, and this one is intended for the protection of our neighbour's reputation. God and man, in fact, are equally the victims of the human tongue, and both need to be guarded against its ravages. We have seen in the last two commandments how it is possible to injure people with our hands, by killing and stealing. This commandment reminds us that it is also possible to injure them with our tongues. Commandment number eight deals with dishonest action, and this one, in its broadest application, deals with dishonest speech.

I—PERJURY

To 'bear false witness' is what today we call 'perjury', and this means the wilful utterance of false evidence while on oath. In civilized countries this is regarded as a most serious offence, and it is obvious that if people were allowed to get away with perjury, then the whole foundation of justice would be undermined. People's reputation and perhaps also their fate would be in the hands of any unscrupulous person who chose to tell lies about them. It stands to reason that the perjurer, if he is caught, is liable to very severe punishment.

But as we have already seen, crimes like murder, theft and perjury often grow from things which, although not criminal, are definitely sinful by Christian standards; and the man who wants to be sure not 'to lay perjury upon his soul' must build several fences to keep himself from the edge of the cliff.

II—SLANDER

Slander, too, can be a civil offence, and people can be awarded very heavy damages if they can prove that things have been said about them by someone else which have injured their character or reputation. In fact the chief difference between perjury and slander is that in the case of perjury the false statement is made under oath, while in the case of slander it is made out of court. Of course, a great deal of slander is allowed to go unchallenged, simply because the slandered person does not want the expense and publicity which would follow legal action; or because he never actually hears the slanderous remarks, which are made to a third person and not to him direct.

It is not very often that a man will deliberately invent a story about another person, knowing it to be untrue, even if he intensely dislikes that person. More often than not slander begins as a story about someone which is repeated, embroidered, twisted, enlarged and finally believed as a piece of factual truth. Anyone who has a hand in its production is to some extent guilty of slander.

III—GOSSIP

One of the most popular breeding grounds for slander is gossip, idle and unnecessary chatter about other people and their affairs. It always gives us pleasure to be first with the news, and if that news concerns another person, it seems to be doubly worth passing on. 'Have you heard about poor old Michael?' we ask, in the tone of voice which suggests we will be only too glad to supply any lack of information. 'No,' comes the reply, 'what has happened to him?' Then follows the spicy piece of gossip. 'Poor old Michael,' we tell our friend, is in trouble with the police, or had had a row with his parents, or his wife, or is in danger of being sacked from his school or his job.

When we think about it afterwards, it is hard to see what has been gained by our passing on this information. Our friend has derived no benefit, because he has been loaded a little earlier than he need have been with a distressing piece of news about someone he knows. 'Poor old Michael' himself has certainly not benefited, because his reputation, already tarnished, has now been tarnished a little more. And what have I gained? Nothing at all, except the unworthy, unchristian pleasure of spreading a little scandal.

IV—EXAGGERATION

No one will begrudge the good story-teller the right to embroider and embellish what he has to say, and no one will take him too seriously; but the trouble begins when we do not check the habit when talking about other people. It is like that game in which a message is passed down a line from mouth to mouth, and the result is then compared ludicrously with the original. And there are some people who you know will exaggerate what you tell them. In no time a broken leg has been amputated, a puncture has become a serious accident, and a sick relative is dead and buried. It has its funny side, of course; but not where other people's characters or reputations are concerned, where it can lead to the most damaging slander.

V—RUMOUR

In any society there are bound to be rumours, but the danger arises when they are passed on to other people as pieces of factual truth. This is really another form of exaggeration, and can lead to great embarrassment and distress. It is always the Christian's duty to try to establish the truth of what he is saying, or to make it quite clear that it is in fact only a rumour. To pass a rumour off as truth can be a most malicious thing to do.

VI—LYING

The most obvious form of verbal dishonesty of course, is the lie, and this is at the back of much of what we have been saying. Over and over again this is condemned in the Bible (Revelation 21. 27), and no doubt most of us from childhood have been urged always to tell the truth. Nothing disrupts society more quickly or more radically than untruthfulness. It used to be said that 'an Englishman's word is his bond'. We must hope that that is still generally true, for how can trade or commerce or business flourish or indeed survive if we do not know whether someone is telling the truth or not?

George Washington had the reputation of never having told a lie ('Father, I cannot tell a lie. I did it with my little hatchet'), and if so, he must be just about the only person who has avoided this prevalent and contagious disease. David said in the heat of the moment, all men are liars (Psalm 116. 11), but I am inclined to think he is right and Jesus seemed to think so, too (John 8. 44).

But a lie need not mean the deliberate telling of an untruth. It can take different and more subtle forms. If I allow someone else's lie to go unchallenged, I am nearly as guilty as if I told that lie myself. I am 'an accessory after the fact', as they call the man who helps to dispose of the body after a murder. It is very easy to do this. We are at a party and we hear one or two people running down a third person whom we know. In the end we hear them say something about him which is quite untrue. It is tempting to let it go, especially if we do not happen to like the person concerned, and if we want to keep in with the people who are discussing him. But we ought not to do so. We ought to come to his rescue. We ought to say, 'Oh! come now, I know Jack takes his cricket a bit seriously, but he never called the umpire a ———'.

Again, we can tell a lie by withholding part of the truth. A witness in court promises to speak 'the truth, *the whole truth,* and nothing but the truth'. A half-truth can be more dangerous than a lie, and sometimes it is our duty as Christians to supply that last little piece which will turn the jigsaw puzzle into a picture, and give a fairer impression of someone's character or reputation.

In an earlier chapter we thought of those occasions when to tell a lie appears to be the lesser of two evils. It is my belief that they are very rare, and we must be careful not to use this excuse for avoiding personal embarrassment. There is really no such thing as a 'white lie', and Byron was guilty of a very dangerous euphemism when he said, 'And after all what is a lie? 'Tis but the truth in masquerade.'

. . . . . .

'If any man offend not in word,' says James, 'the same is a perfect man, and able also to bridle the whole body.' (James 3. 2). How right he was! The trouble lies with the tongue. We have already considered this in some detail, but here are one or two further reflections.

The tongue is very small, like a rudder. In the normal way, and in polite society, the tongue, like the rudder, is unseen. But what an influential thing it is! It determines the whole course of a person's life. Just as a small key can open a great gate, so six inches of pink flesh can have the most colossal influence. During the last war a poster appeared everywhere which said, 'Careless talk costs lives'. It was a reminder that some stray remark about when a ship sailed, or a soldier rejoined his unit, could get back to the enemy, and result in great harm to our cause. So it is with us. The malicious, backbiting tongue can do untold damage.

The tongue is very sharp, like a sword. Sometimes we speak, don't we, about a 'cutting remark'? We mean that we can hurt people's feelings with our tongues, and damage, not their bodies, but their minds and their personalities. 'Many have fallen by the edge of the sword; but not so many as have fallen by the tongue', says the writer of Ecclesiasticus. It is like driving nails into a plank. When we apologize, we pull the nails out again; but what about the holes?

Of course, there are times when it is right and

proper to use the sword. Jesus used it on many occasions, and said some very sharp things to the scribes and the Pharisees. It is sometimes our duty to speak against people, and to warn others of their influence. We must not shirk this duty. To avoid slander, gossip and so on does not mean that we must never rebuke evil when we see it. Of course we must.

The tongue is very strong, like a wild beast. The tongue has been 'born free', and it is a life's work to tame it and train it to behave properly. We cannot do it by ourselves. The tongue needs a 'keeper'; and as we thought earlier on, there is only one Person who can look after it for us. We shall need constantly to ask His help. Without that help, it will always be breaking loose, and causing trouble.

The tongue has a very close friend and ally—the ear. It is nearly always what we hear that we pass on, and if we can 'tune in' as far as possible to the things that are 'of good report' (Philippians 4. 8), then the tongue will have less unpleasant material to work with. Try to become the sort of Christian in whose presence the rumour dissolves, the lie just can't be told, and the gossip or slander shrivel up. If you hear no evil, then you will not be so tempted to speak any evil. Now and then we meet a Christian like that; but they are very rare.

12. IF ONLY I HAD...

From deeds (murder, adultery, theft) via words (false witness) we come finally to thoughts. Does it strike you as strange that 'covetousness' should be the one thing mentioned? Are there not even more serious sins, even in the realm of thought, such as pride, for example, or impurity? The reason why covetousness is forbidden so expressly is because it is often the cause of the other things which we have been considering. Again and again we find it condemned in the Bible, far more often than murder, adultery and theft, because so often when the reason for these other things has been discovered, it is found to be covetousness.

What is covetousness? The dictionary has several words for it—greed, avarice, cupidity. It is that eager, restless desire to possess what we have not got, even if it happens to belong to someone else. It is what I have called elsewhere the spirit of acquisitiveness. One way in which it shows itself is in that curious desire to 'keep up with the Joneses'. When we are young, we feel we must at any cost have a bicycle as good as John Jones's, or a dress as expensive and pretty as Mary Jones's. As we get older, it is Mr. Jones's motor mower, car, garden or house that we begin to want to have; or Mrs. Jones's elaborate kitchen equipment.

Of course, it is very unlikely to lead to an organized attack on the Jones family, and running off with all their possessions. But it probably will lead to envious glances over the garden fence, to jealous little hints and remarks, and even to the injuring of good neighbourly relations. ('We don't speak to the Joneses now. They are so stuck up.') It could also lead to a more grasping desire for money, and a readiness to get it by ways which are not too honest.

Looking through the Bible, it is sad to see how many crimes have been due to covetousness of one sort or another. The first occasion, you will remember, was when a dishonest gardener stole his master's fruit—or rather his wife did, and shared it with him (Genesis 3. 6). What made them do it? The fruit was not theirs, and they had been told not to touch it; but it looked good, and they knew that in some mysterious way it would make them wise. We are told that they wanted to be 'as gods'. It was like keeping up with the Joneses, and it led to theft.

Then there was Achan. Do you remember him? (Joshua 7. 19-21). He was told to destroy all the enemy property. There was to be no looting, on pain of death. But he disobeyed. He kept a whole lot of money, and a beautifully embroidered gown. Perhaps he excused himself that it was for Mrs. A., but he took it and hid it, and then lied about it. In the end he was caught and punished. It all began with greed. What was his excuse? 'I saw ... I coveted ... I took ...'.

Let us move on to David. How I love David! He was a sort of Old Testament Peter, so vital, and yet so vulnerable. He was a shepherd, soldier, poet, king—he had the lot. What more could he possibly want? Poor David! He had one great weakness. His neighbour, Uriah, was at the front, fighting for his country. David ought to have been there himself, but for some reason he was not, and was taking his ease at home, while his armies were besieging Rabbah. One evening, as he walked on the housetop, he saw Uriah's wife, and 'the woman was very beautiful to look upon' (2 Samuel 11). There followed enquiries, invitations, assignations... There followed also the most tragic and sordid chapter in the life of that great and good man, a chapter which he never ceased to regret. How did it all begin? He saw, he coveted, he took....

Move on now many hundreds of years. Here is a man who is ambitious and greedy, and who has the reputation of being light-fingered. One day he hears of a chance to make quite a large sum of money. It is just a matter of telling the authorities where they can find his leader, and delivering Him into their hands (Matthew 26. 14-16). 'They are sure to find Him before long anyway,' he excused himself as he pocketed the money, 'I am only hastening on the inevitable.' And so covetousness led to the murder of Jesus, and the ruin of Judas; for 'Still as of old, man by himself is priced; for thirty pieces Judas sold *himself, not Christ.*'

The eleventh chapter of the book of Hebrews has been called 'The Westminster Abbey of the Bible'. As you move through it, you come upon verse after verse which records the exploits of some great men of faith. We might also compose a 'Rogues' Gallery'. We've seen some of its members already. There are several other candidates—Gehazi, Ananias, Sapphira—and the trouble with them all was that they broke the tenth commandment. They coveted what was not theirs; and in doing so they went on to commit murder, adultery and theft.

Of course, not every case of covetousness will turn into one of these poisonous things, just as not every egg will produce a chicken. But it could do so, and we simply must not give it the chance. Anyway, the commandment makes it quite clear that the spirit of covetousness is sinful in itself, quite apart from the things it may lead to. It betrays an unChrist-like spirit.

I—A MATERIALISTIC SPIRIT

The covetous person shows that his mind is centred on this world. In Paul's graphic phrase, 'his god is his belly' (Philippians 3. 19). In other words, his horizon is bounded by *things*—food, drink, money, sex, possessions, pleasures and so on. These things dominate his life, and, in seeking and trying to find them, he hopes to discover true happiness.

But God made us for something much better than that. Man is not a physical creature only, like the animals, but he has been endowed with a spirit, which must seek and find Him. There once died a very rich banker, and he was given a lavish funeral. Unfortunately, in one of the hymns there was a misprint, and instead of saying 'Land *me* safe on Canaan's side', it went as follows: 'Land *my* safe on Canaan's side.' That is the one thing we cannot do. 'We brought nothing into this world, and it is certain that we can carry nothing out' (1 Timothy 6. 7). Two men were discussing a friend who had recently died. 'I hear he left quarter of a million,' said one of them. 'Is that so?' replied the other man, 'and what did he take with him?'

Jesus told a vivid little story to underline this lesson. A certain farmer prospered greatly, in fact so much so that he felt he could retire at once, and live comfortably on his profits. So he settled down to enjoy what his industry and thrift had brought him, with never a thought for God, or for the welfare of his own soul. 'But,' we read, 'God said unto him, Thou fool, this night thy soul shall be required of thee ...' (Luke 12. 13-21). The man had made three mistakes. He thought he was being wise, but God called him a *fool*. He thought of his body, but God was interested in his *soul*. He thought he had plenty of time, but God called him *this night*.

II—A DISCONTENTED SPIRIT

Here is the second reason why covetousness is wrong, quite apart from what it may lead to. It shows a discontented spirit. The writer to the Hebrews says, 'Be content with such things as ye have; for He hath said, I will never leave thee nor forsake thee' (Hebrews 13. 5). The Christian is someone who has learnt contentment, not because he has a great abundance of material possessions, but because he has learnt to enjoy the friendship of Christ. He is able to say with St. Paul, 'I have learned, in whatsoever state I am, therewith to be content'. (Philippians 4. 11).

It is the way of the world to imagine that peace and contentment are to be found at the top. 'If I can only get *there*,' says someone, 'all will be well. Once I've got a place in that team, once I've got a seat on the Board, I shall be happy.' Then again there is the desire for the larger car or the better house—things which must be sought and obtained, not because they are necessary, or bring any great advantage to family life, but for their own sakes, and because it is fondly hoped they will make us happier. But do they? Jesus said, 'The meek shall inherit the earth' (Matthew 5. 5). They cannot buy it or conquer it or win it, but they can inherit it; because they have discovered the secret of enjoying what they have, in fact, no desire to possess; 'having nothing', therefore, 'they possess all things' (2 Corinthians 6. 10).

True contentment is to be found in Jesus Christ: the contentment which comes from knowing that He has died for us, and forgiven all our sins; the contentment that comes from having Him as our constant companion; the contentment that comes from His word and His promises. So many seek contentment in material things, and covet their neighbour's ox and ass, motor-bike and television set, garden and yacht. I am not suggesting that these things are not pleasant to have. Of course they are! They add to the variety and enjoyment of life. They are like sugar cakes. But Jesus said, 'I am the bread of life' (John 6. 35). We can get on without cakes, but we must have bread. It is the staff of life. If God sees fit to send us the cakes, well and good, but they are not worth queuing for. They are not worth too much sweat and toil. They sweeten life, but they do not satisfy.

III—A SELFISH SPIRIT

The covetous man is by definition a selfish man. Having taken so much trouble to accumulate wealth or reach a certain position of eminence, he is going to hug his achievements to himself. Such an attitude is not only the very negation of Christian love, but the height of folly, because he is thereby depriving himself of the happiness which comes from sharing what he possesses with others.

One of the great paradoxes of the Christian life was stated by Jesus when He said, 'Happiness lies more in giving than receiving' (Acts 20. 35). The man who is generous with his time, his money, his advice and his sympathy is going to reap rich dividends of friendship and love; for it is equally true in the spiritual realm as in any other, that 'a man reaps what he sows' (Galatians 6. 7).

No one demonstrated this more completely than Jesus Himself. Equality with God was within His grasp, but He refused to snatch at it (Philippians 2. 5-8), sacrificing everything He had—position, reputation and life itself—out of love for us, and for the joy of restoring us to His Father.

On the tomb of the Earl of Devon who died in 1419, and was buried at Tiverton, you will find this epitaph, and it forms an apt summary of what we have been saying.

> 'What we gave, we have;
> What we spent, we had;
> What we kept, we lost.'

13. THE ENVIRONMENTAL PROBLEM

The standard of living which people enjoy is directly dependent on two things—the economy and the environment. There is a large number of social reforms which we would all like to see, but again and again we run up against a shortage of money. Mysterious things like the 'balance of payments', the 'gold and dollar reserves', 'bank rate' and so on haunt our lives, with the result that houses, schools, hospitals and roads do not get built as fast as they should.

Our other problem is the environment. Chemical fertilizers, industrial waste and sewage disposal are just some of the things which threaten to pollute our air and land, rivers and seas; and unless pretty radical steps are taken in the fairly near future, England will no longer be the 'green and pleasant land' of Blake's imagination.

Now all this is a parable of the spiritual life; for the Christian who earnestly desires to maintain a high standard of moral living finds himself up against the same problems. There is first of all the innate weakness of his human nature, a kind of moral law of gravity which pulls him down whenever he strives to climb. This is something he has got to learn to live with. Like this country, the Christian is not self-supporting. He has no power in himself to help himself, and is wholly dependent upon the presence of Christ in his heart to strengthen and uphold him.

Even the best of Christians experience this tension, and Paul wrote vividly about it in Romans 7. 14-25. He was conscious of this force within him, his old sinful nature striving against his desire to keep the law of God. Victory lies not in the eradication of this force, but in the exercise of one which is greater, namely the power of Christ who lives within. Paul calls it 'the law of the Spirit of life' (Romans 8. 2); for just as the eagle flies aloft, not by eliminating the law of gravity, but by counteracting it with a higher law of life, so the Christian can overcome the law of sin by the living presence in his heart of the Spirit of Christ.

But there is this second problem. We live in a polluted world, and unless we are careful, contamination can reach us through our moral and spiritual environment. Here again the secret of success does not lie, as some have thought, in escapism. The mediaeval answer to this problem was isolation, monasticism. You insulate yourself in a spiritual community from the sordid influences of the world, but while in this way you may preserve your own sanctity, you cut very little ice.

On the other hand the opposite extreme is just as unsatisfactory. There are those who become so identified with the world in which they live that they undermine their own spiritual health and destroy any influence they might have had. The salt is just as useless if it loses its flavour through contamination with other things as it is if you leave it isolated in the salt-cellar (Matthew 5. 13).

Somewhere between these two extremes lies the balance we must strive for. We must be 'in the world', but at the same time not 'of it' (John 17. 15). The ship must be in the sea, but the sea has no business in the ship. Jesus achieved this balance. He was known as 'the friend of sinners' (Matthew 11. 19), but no one ever mistook Him for a sinner, and those who watched Him realized that though never isolating from them He was never identified with them, and described Him as being 'separate from sinners' (Hebrews 7. 26).

No Christian can, or should try to, escape the environment in which God has placed him. But what do we mean by our 'environment'? It is those things which give a moral shape or pattern to our lives, and which influence us spiritually, just as we are influenced physically by the air we breathe and the food we eat. Basically these things are good; for 'every prospect pleases, and only man is vile', and their influence can be wholly beneficial. But often they have become polluted by man himself, and then their influence is wholly bad. There are at least four ingredients in our moral and spiritual environment.

Possessions. The Bible nowhere condemns money nor people for making or earning it, but it does warn us of the dangers attached to it, and it speaks out strongly against 'the love of money' (1 Timothy 6. 10), and making wealth our ambition. Where the Christian's standards should be beyond reproach is in the way he gets his money and his motives for getting it.

It goes without saying that no Christian will stoop to dishonest or fraudulent ways of making money; at least it should go without saying, but the lure of wealth can be so strong that even Christians can be snared into financial deception, to their own shame and the dishonour of their Master, and need to be on their guard.

It is in this context of making money that we ought to think for a moment about gambling. It has been said that everyone is at heart a gambler, and there is probably some truth in that. We love taking a risk, and the excitement involved; and would we ever have reached the South Pole, climbed Mount Everest, landed on the moon, or heard the Gospel, if men and women had not been prepared to hazard their lives?

It is not the presence of this spirit that is wrong, but its misuse; and Christians have always disapproved of gambling with money. Why? First, it breeds and encourages that covetous, acquisitive desire to get something for nothing, and this in turn makes people idle and parasitical. Secondly, the gambler can only make money at someone else's expense. People have been ruined by gambling, and it is no answer to say that they were not obliged to take the risk. They ought not to have been tempted to do so. It takes two to gamble. In the third place a Christian tries to regard himself as a steward of money which has been lent him by God, and not as the outright owner. Therefore he feels that it is not really his to play with, any more than he would gamble with the funds of some charitable organization of which he was treasurer.

If these arguments are sound, and I think from a Christian point of view they are, it will obviously colour our approach to the many different money-raising efforts that are used today—raffles, premium bonds, 'one-armed bandits' and the like. To what extent do they offer short-cuts to wealth, or encourage an avaricious spirit and too great a respect for mere chance?

Someone may say, 'What about the Stock Exchange?' There are those who use this as a gambling machine, getting 'in' in the morning and 'out' in the afternoon, and hoping to make a profit in the interval. But the vast majority of people use the Stock Exchange as a means of investment, expecting a reasonable return for their money and hoping that the original capital will appreciate. In doing this they are doing much the same as people who buy and sell cars, cattle, fruit and pictures at a time when it is most to their advantage to do so.

But the Christian will also try to keep his motives for getting money pure. He should not want it simply to hoard, or to spend on luxuries, or necessarily to improve his own standard of living or that of his family, but rather to increase his capacity to do good on as wide a scale as possible.

The Jews made it a rule to 'tithe' their income, that is to say, the first tenth was given to God. Even in these days of high taxation, this is an excellent principle to adopt, and we ought when budgeting to make sure that God is given the first cut off the joint and not the last.

Our giving ought to be intelligent as well as generous. That is to say, we should make full use of those means which exist whereby income tax can be recovered on gifts covenanted to charitable organisations. Any Christian accountant will be able to advise us on these matters.

There is no harm in making money and in earning as much as we can. John Wesley urged his followers to 'Get all you can, and save all you can,' but he was careful to add, 'and give all you can.' And how splendidly he lived up to this rule! When he earned £50 a year, he found he could live on £30 and so he gave away £20. When his income went up to £100 a year, he still found he could live on £30 a year, and so he gave away £70!

Christian work depends for its support upon committed Christians. If we don't help, we can expect no one else to do so. God loves a cheerful giver (2 Corinthians 9. 7), and there are few things which can make us more cheerful than to know the joy and happiness our money can sometimes purchase for other people.

Friendships. We cannot live without friends any more than we can live without money, but once again they belong to this neutral zone. They can be the greatest possible blessing to us, and they can be an unmitigated curse. Someone has said that while we are given our relations, we can choose our own friends, and the wise man is he who surrounds himself with the sort who will be a challenge and a comfort to him, and help to deepen his faith in God.

This is not to say that he won't be friendly with everyone he meets, but a Christian will reserve those confidences and intimacies which can only be shared with a close friend for one who has the same values, principles and standards as himself. We all meet people of whom we can say, 'it does me good to be in that person's company', and this is the kind of friend we shall be fortunate to cultivate; for 'a good friend is the medicine of life'.

But medicine is sometimes unpleasant to the taste, and the best friends will not be those who always tell us what we want to know. They will stand up to us at times, and tell us the truth, however unpalatable this may be. If we are sensible we shall not resent this, and will remember that 'faithful are the wounds of a friend' (Proverbs 27. 6). We don't want to surround ourselves with a lot of 'Yes-men', like the committee whose chairman complained that all he had was a 'Sevenfold Amen'.

We are warned in the Bible not to be 'unequally yoked together with unbelievers' (2 Corinthians 6. 14), and while this is rightly taken to apply in the first instance to marriage, and the tragedy of a spiritual *mésalliance*, we ought not to overlook the danger of forming any close business association or partnership with those who do not see eye-to-eye with us on the fundamental matters of faith and morals.

Pleasures. Everyone needs leisure and relaxation, but here again the Christian will exercise discretion in his choice of entertainment. It is true that God 'giveth us richly all things to enjoy' (1 Timothy 6. 17), but some of those things, noble and worthy in themselves, have become polluted, and for the sake of our own souls are best avoided where possible.

There are books and magazines, films, plays and TV shows which seem to be almost deliberately designed to inflame sexual passions or to encourage violence and cruelty. Most of us know our own selves well enough to realize that these feelings want little encouragement before they begin to get out of hand, and if we are wise, we shall be fairly strict with ourselves when it comes to choosing what we read or look at.

It isn't that any of the mass media are bad in

themselves, but simply that man has polluted them so often, just as he has so often turned green fields and woods into a concrete desert; and where these things are concerned the Christian has the difficult threefold duty of avoiding what is evil, enjoying what is good and trying to reclaim what is remediable.

Of course, where any form of pleasure is concerned—a game, a hobby, an art—the Christian needs to watch the inroads it makes upon his time, his thought and his ambitions. It is all too easy to make a god out of a game, for example, and in these days of highly developed professionalism, it is more difficult for the Christian to excel in sport and still to keep his priorities right.

Work. This leads into the fourth part of our environment—our work. People's jobs affect them in different ways. Let me mention two dangers connected with our daily work. First, there is boredom. There are many people who are condemned, if that is the word, to doing what in a few years' time will be done by a piece of machinery. Their task in life is soulless, mechanical and tedious in the extreme.

It is easy to advise such people not to worry, but to regard their work as a means to an end, the end being the ever-increasing amount of leisure which the modern worker is able to enjoy. I can't help feeling that this is a second-best view. Work ought to be more than a money-earning operation, and I think the Christian should find in even the dullest job, the joy of work well done, of skilled precision, and the feeling that in some sense he is co-operating with the Creator in the development and exploitation of the earth and all that is in it. I think this must be what Paul meant when he urged his readers, some of whom were slaves; 'Whatever you are doing, put your whole heart into it, as if you were doing it for the Lord and not for men' (Colossians 3. 23).

There is a danger of making a false dichotomy between work which is sacred and profane, spiritual and non-spiritual. All work is glorifying to God if it is done in the right spirit. As George Herbert reminds us, 'Nothing can be so mean which with this tincture —"For Thy sake" will not grow bright and clean.'

It is worth saying too that even the most spiritual callings have their 'chores'. With the best will in the world, no parson can spend his whole time preaching, writing or visiting. There is much administration to be done, and no one should despise it, for it provides the framework for evangelistic and pastoral activities.

But the danger of allowing oneself to be bored is that it flows over into our family and social life in the form of bitterness and frustration. The happy man is the one who has found a job which absorbs as much of him as possible, and is worthy of his intelligence, his energy and his training.

The other danger is the exact opposite, that is to say, a man who finds his job too absorbing, who becomes perhaps an obsessive worker, who is, as we say, 'married to his work'. This can have a very disruptive effect upon his home life, and very easily supplant the time and thought he ought to be giving to his family, his friends and his church.

We must beware of what has been called the 'barrenness of the busy life'. Martha suffered from this. She had to be 'at it' all the time (Luke 10. 38-42), and spread about an atmosphere of feverish restlessness.

A Christian also needs to be careful about ambition. It is possible to be so keen on one's work, so rightly anxious to succeed and reach the top, that principles and standards begin to slip, unworthy methods are employed, and a man ends up by selling his soul for his job. Cronin's famous best-selling novel *The Citadel* provides a fascinating study of a doctor who did just this.

Possessions, friends, pleasures and work—these things comprise the atmosphere, the environment in which we have to live. There is no escaping, no immunization, but there is an element of choice. We need not stay in polluted areas or swim in contaminated lakes and rivers, and the progress and success of our spiritual lives will largely depend upon the wisdom with which we exercise this freedom of choice.

14. THE GOLDEN RULE

THE whole of the Ten Commandments are summed up for us in one sentence by Jesus Himself: 'Thou shalt love the Lord thy God with all thy heart, and with all thy soul, and with all thy strength, and with all thy mind; and thy neighbour as thyself' (Luke 10. 27). In other words, love is the golden rule for fulfilling all the other rules, for there is not one of the Ten Commandments which love will allow us to break; while at the same time without the Ten Commandments we would not know what love involved.

The relationship between Love and Law may be expressed by saying that Love provides the motive for pleasing God and Law provides the means. It is because we love God that we want to obey His law, and it is by obeying it that we show that we love Him.

But it would be a great mistake to suppose that love simply means a kind of Christian 'work to rule'—a careful observance of the letter of the law but little regard for its spirit. Love works overtime. It doesn't just avoid slander, it spreads the truth. It prefers to give rather than to lend, and if compelled to go one mile, it will volunteer to go two (Matthew 5. 38-42).

For a proper understanding of Christian love we cannot do better than turn to the thirteenth chapter of Paul's first letter to the Corinthians, the whole of which is devoted to this subject. He begins by stressing the supremacy of love over everything else (1-3); he continues with an analysis of love, breaking it up like light into all the colours of the rainbow (4-7); and he ends by emphasizing the permanence of love compared with the transience of other things (8-13).

I—THE SUPREMACY OF LOVE

Think of the most gifted Christian imaginable, a man with rare understanding and deep faith, eloquent, persuasive and impressive. Unless these gifts are bathed in love for God and compassion for his fellow men, they are just hollow, empty noises. Paul certainly did not underestimate spiritual gifts. The whole of the previous chapter is devoted to them, and he urged his readers to desire earnestly the best of these gifts. But without love, they are worth nothing.

Or think of another kind of Christian. This man is remarkable not so much for what he has received as for what he has given. He lives a life of generosity and sacrifice. He is a philanthropist and a martyr, but unless his motive has been one of genuine love, his achievements are absolutely nil.

Love is the greatest thing in the world. Just as the sunshine after heavy rain gives the whole countryside a new complexion, so love transforms what we are and what we do. But what is this mysterious quality —love? How can we understand and measure it?

II—THE ANALYSIS OF LOVE

In the next few verses (4-7), Paul gives us what we might call a photograph of love. He begins with a *negative*. Perhaps it is a commentary on the sinfulness of human nature that so many Christian virtues have to be defined for us negatively. 'Love envieth not; love vaunteth not itself, is not puffed up, doth not behave itself unseemly, seeketh not her own, is not easily provoked, thinketh no evil, rejoiceth not in iniquity.'

The Christian needs to develop a good, strong negative, and paradoxically love begins by hating. 'Ye that love the Lord,' says the psalmist, 'hate evil' (Psalm 97. 10). The Christian has to be a good hater, Paul provides us with a list of things with which we can begin. It makes pretty grim reading: jealousy, vanity, pride, rudeness, selfishness, touchiness, suspicion, malevolence.

But while the Christian must hate evil, he should have nothing but love in his heart for the evil-doer. He must always distinguish between the sin and the sinner, and our hatred of evil must never prevent us from extending the loving, sympathetic hand to those who have succumbed to temptation—the unmarried mother, the prisoner, the moral outcast, the drug addict.

This is what it means when it says, 'rejoiceth not in iniquity', or 'is not pleased when others go wrong'; for we are told that 'love covereth all sins' (Proverbs 10. 12). Sir Edwin Landseer (who was Queen Victoria's favourite painter) once spent a day turning a dark brown coffee stain on some beautiful new wall paper in the house where he was staying into a mural landscape; and when the guests returned in the evening they found that the tragic blemish had not only been covered but transformed. 'Where sin abounded, grace did much more abound' (Romans

5. 20). That is how God loves us, and wants us to love others.

Paul now turns from the negative to the positive side of love, and gives us a *picture*. 'Love suffereth long, and is kind.' In other words, he shows us the two moods of love—passive and active. Patience (long-suffering) suggests the normal attitude of love: love at ease, love off duty, calmly accepting life as it comes with its trials and tribulations. Love isn't easily 'put out'. It isn't irritated by a sudden change of plan, or by a domestic crisis, a disturbing letter, or an unwelcome visitor. Love has time for everyone and for everything.

Then we have love in its active mood—'Love is kind'. This time it is not resting, but working, and looking for things to do. A famous Headmaster, J. F. Roxburgh, speaking about his own schooldays, said that what he remembered about other boys was not whether they were clever or athletic, but whether they were kind. Surely no one can ask for a better reason for being remembered than that! For 'kind hearts are more than coronets.'

It is interesting how perfectly we see these two qualities—patience and kindness—in the life of Jesus. Faced with the opposition of the authorities, the dullness of His disciples and the unceasing demands of the crowd, He never grew irritable, and was always at leisure to listen, to help and to explain. And think how kind He was! A great deal of His time was spent just doing good turns to people. From first to last He thought of others before Himself— from the moment when the wine ran out at a wedding and He came to the rescue (John 2) to His words of thoughtful concern upon the cross.

But Paul is not content with the picture as it is. He gives us an *enlargement*. He wants to show us that there is no breaking-point for love. It 'beareth all things, believeth all things, hopeth all things, endureth all things. Love never faileth.' There is no test it cannot pass; no strain it will not bear.

Bearing and enduring. There is a subtle difference between these two words in the original Greek. To 'bear' means to 'put up with', and to 'endure' means to 'face up to'. In other words, love accepts what it cannot change. It bears with 'the slings and arrows of outrageous fortune'. But it also faces up to the challenge of what can be changed. When necessary it will 'take arms against a sea of troubles.' It has declared war on evil, and won't tolerate the march of injustice, dishonesty and greed.

Believing and hoping—faith and hope. Faith is concerned with the present, and hope with the future. Faith has complete trust in God to meet our daily needs; and hope looks to Him for the future fulfilment of what He has promised. Love therefore is the final answer to the deepest human needs, because it has total confidence in the goodness and the sovereignty of God.

III—THE PERMANENCE OF LOVE

In the closing verses Paul returns to the contrast between gifts and graces which we noted earlier. Gifts have their uses, but also their limitations. The gift of prophecy, for instance, may help us in our Christian witness in this life, but when we graduate to the next life, we shall not need it, but will put it away like a toy we used when we were children. The gift of understanding may help us to solve some of the riddles which we find in this life, but when I come face to face with Christ, my knowledge will be as complete as His knowledge of me, and I shall need that gift no more.

· · · · · ·

This then is the golden rule for Christian living: 'Thou shalt love the Lord thy God ... and thy neighbour ... as thyself.' Notice the grammar, because it is different from what we normally learn, but very important: 'Thy God ... thy neighbour ... thyself.' The first person is God, the second person is our neighbour, and the third person ourselves.

But one final question remains. How do we get that love? Where does it come from? The answer is of course that it is not generated from within ourselves—not original, but derived; for 'we love, because He first loved us' (1 John 4. 19). His love is the cause of ours.

It happens in two ways. We are told that part of the work of God's Holy Spirit is to 'shed abroad in our hearts' the love of God (Romans 5. 5). Just as by pulling back the curtains of a darkened room, you allow the sunshine to fill every corner of it with light and warmth, so when Jesus Christ comes to live within our hearts by His Holy Spirit He begins to warm them with love for God. 'I felt my heart strangely warmed', wrote John Wesley when, on May 24, 1738, he trusted Christ fully for the first time, and experienced the infusion of His Holy Spirit.

But it is also a process of reflection, for as we think about Christ, looking upon Him and taking Him as our example, we shall find that slowly but surely we are changed into a likeness of Himself (2 Corinthians 3. 18). Nathanael Hawthorne tells us of the village legend that one day a great leader would arise whose features would resemble those carved by nature in the rocks overlooking its streets and houses. The story fired the imagination of a boy named Ernest who used to sit day after day gazing at the figure, dreaming dreams about the future. Many years went by, false leaders came and went, and then one day when he rose to address the people, they recognized the astonishing likeness of Ernest to the great stone face, and he was acclaimed as the long-expected leader. He had been changed by beholding.

some of the other books
by John Eddison
published by Scripture Union

THE TROUBLED MIND

To experience doubt or fear, loneliness or anxiety, unhappiness or discouragement, is part of being human. What makes us different is not whether we have these experiences, but how we cope with them. John Eddison writes positively, applying the central truths of the Christian faith to these states of mind, and recalling that the Bible describes people like ourselves 'warts and all'. This is a book for all temperaments, for it will not only encourage the more sensitive, but also help the extrovert to be more aware of other peoples' problems.

IT'S A GREAT LIFE

'It's a great life,' says the author from his own experience as a Christian. But it is not only experience which qualifies John Eddison to write this book; it is also his widely acknowledged gift for explaining Christian truths clearly. And it is with all his usual clarity that he talks about the adventure of the Christian life.

'What's new?' he asks, and 'How can I be sure I am a Christian?' He also talks specifically about times of doubt and failure. And there are chapters on service and vocation, on prayer and Bible reading, and on the Christian Church, the worldwide family of believers.

WHAT MAKES A LEADER?

The lives of the great are always fascinating. Is there a recipe for greatness? What makes a man an outstanding leader?

In *What Makes a Leader?* John Eddison asks questions like this about ten top people from the pages of the Bible — men like Joseph, once a spoiled child and very conceited, who emerged from prison to become Prime Minister of Egypt; and like Moses, who became one of the most remarkable leaders of all time.

This book has been given an extra dimension by the inclusion of questions at the end of each chapter — questions to think over and which can be discussed in a group.